THE LEISURE ENVIRONMENT

Marcus Colquhoun

PITMAN
PUBLISHING

PITMAN PUBLISHING
128 Long Acre, London WC2E 9AN

A Division of Longman Group UK Limited

© Marcus Colquhoun 1993

First published in Great Britain 1993
Reprinted 1993, 1994

British Library Cataloguing-in-Publication Data
A catalogue record for this book is available from the British Library

ISBN 0-273-03752-8

Typeset by Pantek Arts, Maidstone, Kent
Printed in England by Clays Ltd, St Ives plc

The Publishers' policy is to use paper manufactured from sustainable forests.

THE LEISURE ENVIRONMENT

To Glenda, Alex and Simon who have sacrificed so much of their valuable leisure time to provide me with support and encouragement.

CONTENTS

INTRODUCTION

The aim of this book is to provide students on BTEC National Leisure Studies and GNVQ Level 3 Leisure & Tourism courses with an overview of the leisure industry. Many students when they enrol on their leisure studies course have only a very limited knowledge of the scope and scale of the industry; their impression is often that they will learn what it is like to work in a leisure centre and will spend much of their college time playing competitive sports. The reality is very different: during the next two years *you will be studying the business of leisure*.

Leisure and Tourism together represent one of oldest, largest and fastest growing industries in the world.

The book provides an integrated approach to studying the industry. The first chapter, 'The History of Leisure' examines the origins of modern day leisure activities and shows how, particularly since the Industrial Revolution, a leisure industry has evolved. The next three chapters provide students with a core which examines the organisational structures of the industry, communication within those organisations and how they are financed in the public, private and voluntary sectors.

Chapters 5, 6, 7 and 9 consider four specific contexts of the industry: Sport and Physical Recreation, Tourism, Countryside and Art and Entertainment. In these chapters common features of organisation and funding are outlined and the scope of provision in the sectors is examined in greater depth.

'Marketing in the Leisure Industry' (Chapter 8) provides students with an opportunity to examine the 'glamorous' side of leisure as a business and emphasises the importance of providing quality of experience and customer care to leisure customers.

The final chapter 'Working in the Leisure Industry', considers the personal qualities which recruits to the industry should possess and highlights some of the factors which students should consider when embarking on a career in leisure.

Each chapter contains practical assignments which encourage students to find out more about the industry: how and by whom it is organised and funded. The assignments require students to visit leisure facilities, talk to key personnel employed within them, observe what goes on and draw conclusions. In completing these assignments students will be able to develop their business related skills at the same time at they gain a greater understanding of the dynamics of the industry.

The case studies and further assignments, at the end of the book, enable students to broaden their outlook on the industry and to consider it not just in the context of leisure within the community but of the business environment as a whole.

Leisure is a dynamic, challenging and constantly changing environment in which to work and study. By reading this book students will, hopefully, gain sufficient awareness and understanding to be able to rise to the challenges which the leisure industry presents.

CHAPTER 1

THE HISTORY OF LEISURE

OBJECTIVES

On completion of this chapter, students will:

▶ be aware of the nature and importance of leisure in history

▶ understand the social significance of leisure in society

▶ appreciate the technological developments that have shaped leisure in the twentieth century.

Primitive leisure

Imagine living in a world without cars, electricity, books or shopping centres. These are all things that most of us take for granted and which many people feel they cannot do without. They are the products of industrialised society. 'Primitive' people lived without these luxuries, struggling to survive by hunting and gathering, not knowing where their next meal was coming from or where they would sleep for the night. What leisure did these people enjoy?

Leisure in ancient times did exist, but it was different to our understanding of leisure today:

- 'singing' was probably first used as a means of scaring away wild animals and, later, as a way of making labouring in the fields more enjoyable
- dancing was part of the celebrations after a successful hunt,
- leisure time hardly existed except, possibly, during bad weather when crop gathering or hunting was difficult.

In many parts of the world today there are still people who work hard and long to sustain themselves and their families. There is little time for leisure activities for many of the starving people of the Third World. Ironically, our awareness in the West of the constant struggles these people face has been made possible by the most popular leisure activity of the twentieth century – watching television.

■ LEISURE IN ANCIENT TIMES

It was only when societies started to become efficient and produce food surpluses that leisure as we know it started to exist. As cultures advanced, people were allocated different work roles: successful hunters and gatherers became specialists and leaders of their tribes, élite classes developed and leisure became associated with culture, social standing and political status. Some people had time to spare and needed something to fill it.

Leisure in classical, ancient societies, such as Egypt and Babylon, was restricted to three classes of people:

- the nobility
- the military
- religious leaders.

The leisure activities of these rulers included many forms of sport and recreation that still exist today:

- horse racing
- wrestling and boxing
- archery
- dancing
- art
- music
- lavish entertainment.

Traditional activities associated with the need for survival – such as hunting and falconry – became leisure pursuits. Even agriculture became a pleasurable pastime when leisure gardens were created in which the élite members of society could relax.

In ancient Greece, sport was an important part of culture and everyday life. Athletic games were organised as part of religious festivals. In an epic poem written in 700BC, there are references to foot races, longjump contests, javelin and discus throwing – the forerunners of today's track and field athletics. Such was the reputation of the games of ancient Greece that the modern Olympic movement is loosely based on the format that the ancient Greeks adopted.

The main purpose of these ancient competitions, which also included boxing and wrestling contests, was to test military skills: the javelins were spears, the discuses had spikes on them and dancing was taken seriously, being regarded as a form of precision drill that would improve military efficiency. Women were trained to sing and dance and, in one of the provinces, Sparta, where they were expected to do physical exercises, special athletic meetings were organised for women.

In Roman times, leisure meant entertainment: the Roman calendar had as many as 200 days of the year set aside for celebration.

Slaves played music, performed drama, competed in sports, gladiatorial contests, chariot races and staged mock battles. Success meant freedom; failure meant death.

The Colosseum, a stadium in the heart of Rome, had a capacity of over 300 000. The entertainment there was free of charge as the emperors thought it would prevent the masses revolting.

The lavish spectacles attracted people from all over the Roman Empire. The tourists needed accommodation and stalls were set up outside the Colosseum to sell all the visitors souvenirs. Thus, a leisure industry had been created that comprised tourism, hospitality, entertainment and recreation.

It has even been argued that the costs of the lavish entertainments, which increased steadily as the members of the nobility tried to out do one another, contributed to the financial ruin of the Roman Empire.

■ THE DARK AGES

The advent of Christianity and the collapse of the Roman Empire had a major effect on leisure. The very name given to the period between AD400 and 1000, 'The Dark Ages', suggests that life was hard and leisure activities a luxury. Most forms of activity, other than work, were banned for the common people. Any exceptions were linked to 'holy day' celebrations when drinking and gambling were permitted and music and morality plays were performed.

Leisure was also restricted by the social system: labourers were called into the service of their feudal lords either to tend crops or fight. This left them with little time for relaxation. The feudal lords themselves, however, had time on their hands and staged jousting tournaments to test the military skill of their knights and squires.

■ LEISURE IN MEDIEVAL BRITAIN

In medieval Britain (AD1000–1500) leisure was directly related to agricultural life, with religious festivals taking place at key stages of the agricultural year:

- Christmas lasted for 14 days and took place at the time of the Midwinter Feast
- Easter lasted for seven days and corresponded to the pagan Spring Festival
- the autumn harvest became a religious celebration
- labourers celebrated Saint's or 'holy' days and rested on Sundays
- there were many non-religious local festivals ('aledays') and fairs, held in market towns
- leisure meant relaxation and play for the community.

The nobility continued to use leisure as an extension of military training but also turned their attention to the arts. The invention of printing meant that books became available to a wider public (previously reading had been restricted to those who had studied in monasteries or at university; there were few books and they were extremely expensive as they were written out by scribes and beautifully finished).

The church and nobility became increasingly corrupt and licentious. Leisure came to mean gambling, drinking and blood sports, such as cock-fighting and bear-baiting, but this was soon to change.

■ THE REFORMATION

The Reformation in Europe changed not only the church but attitudes to leisure. The church leaders (Martin Luther and John Calvin) upheld the righteous ways of hard work and austerity. Leisure was once again an evil pastime. The 'Protestant work ethic' still exists today where, in some societies, leisure activities are frowned upon, particularly on Sundays.

■ SEVENTEENTH-CENTURY LEISURE

By the seventeenth century, attitudes towards leisure were changing again. The nobility once more were able to enjoy hunting and fishing. They promoted the arts by building stately homes and filling them with beautiful furniture and paintings, commissioning or sponsoring the greatest artists, architects, masons and woodcarvers of the time.

The sons and daughters of the nobility completed their education by going on a 'Grand Tour of Europe'. The original intention of the Grand Tour was to learn to appreciate the arts and the culture of Europe, which the young ladies did, but the young English lords often preferred to regard it as a lengthy, dissolute jaunt. Many of the major towns and cities of Europe developed their tourism facilities on the backs of the high-spending English aristocrats.

■ THE INDUSTRIAL REVOLUTION

The greatest changes took place as a result of the Industrial Revolution.

Mechanisation and mass production encouraged the growth of cities, many people moved out of the small towns and villages to the cities in the hope that they would earn more money than in the country and so have a better life. The reality was very different. The cities became overcrowded and slums developed where people with badly paid jobs lived in areas of poor housing.

In such areas the opportunities for leisure were very restricted: children could not play in the fields; families could not walk in the countryside; the quality of life for the industrial workers was poor and, once again, leisure became a class-based privilege for the few. Leisure was plentiful only for those who could afford it.

Another important development was that the Industrial Revolution created wealth for the middle classes who bought country estates and built luxury town houses where they entertained family and friends. During 'the season' when the cities became too hot for comfort they would visit the Spa Towns such as Bath, Buxton and Tunbridge Wells. The spas were patronised by royalty, whose presence attracted other well-to-do visitors who required accommodation and entertainment during their stay. As the spa towns became popular, they attracted large numbers of less desirable visitors and then the original patrons moved further afield.

By the early part of the nineteenth century, seaside resorts became popular. Doctors advocated sea air and salt water as a cure for all ills. Resorts such as Brighton, Bognor and Broadstairs developed, with luxury hotels and entertainment. Families were able to spend the summer at the seaside. Later in the century the railways were to open up a whole new form of leisure for the masses.

Leisure was still very class based. Landowners hunted with hounds, shot game and fished but tradesmen and apprentices were prohibited from doing so by law. Participation in horse racing, prize fighting and other sports was thought to encourage idleness and laws were passed restricting them.

Traditional rural leisure activities survived and were adapted to meet the changing needs and wants of the people of the cities.

Work in the cities was not limited to daylight hours. Workers had a minimum ten-hour day and six-day week, with Sunday as the day of rest – only the pubs were open.

Figure 1.1 Riding holiday (Courtesy Irish Tourist Board)

The Sabbatarians (an organisation that aimed to keep Sunday as a holy day) promoted the idea of introducing free time for non-devotional leisure. Saturday afternoon became the time when the workers were allowed to play.

Sport in the Industrial Revolution

Football used to be played as a running battle between villages. There was no designated pitch – just some open ground – nor were there any limits on the number of players on a side. It was a form of gang or tribal warfare. This was not possible in the towns, as recreational land was in short supply and the workforce was bound by rules and a timekeeper's clock.

The 'new' football was developed in the public schools, with the aim of channelling pupils' energies in their spare time. It was different because it had rules, penalties for foul play and a time limit. This appealed to employers, spectators and players. Football clubs were formed by companies, local churches, chapels and publicans who frequently provided a pitch on which to play and a changing room for the players.

The following are some notable dates in the history of football:

- the Football Association was founded in 1863
- the first Cup Final of 1871 attracted a gate of 2000
- Blackburn Olympics were the first works team to win the cup in 1883
- the 1900 Cup Final at Crystal Palace had an attendance of 110 802 people.

Football, as a form of urban leisure, had arrived. Leisure, as in Roman times, had become available to all.

Other sports adopted by workers in the late nineteenth century included:

- track and field athletics
- cross country
- rugby football
- cricket
- roller skating
- cycling
- swimming
- lawn tennis
- boxing.

The development of 'modern' sport is often referred to as a demonstration of 'muscular Christianity'. This is because many team sports started in the chapels and churches. Clubs were founded by public school-educated clergymen who were anxious to reduce the amount of drunkenness in the congregation. Other enlightened clergymen were anxious that the people of the new towns and cities should have open spaces for recreation. Land was set aside by the local authorities for playing fields, recreation areas, public baths and gymnasiums. Large stadiums were built on the outskirts of towns and leisure became profitable:

- manufacturers began producing leisure equipment
- events were advertised widely
- trams and railways ran special excursions.

Although most workers were able to relax on Saturday afternoons, this was not the case for people in service industries, who had only Christmas Day and Good Friday as public holidays. This changed with the Bank Holiday Act of 1870. On bank holidays:

- the nation was at leisure
- trains provided cheap transport to the coast
- cities became deserted.

This pleased the church leaders, who were much happier at the prospect of a day at the seaside than a day at the races. By the turn of the century the nation had become leisure orientated: Saturday afternoons meant playing or watching sport; Bank Holidays were for excursions. Further:

- consumers had money in their pockets to spend on leisure
- they were able to travel substantial distances at low cost
- admission charges became a source of revenue
- relaxation continued in the pubs and theatres at dusk
- home-based leisure improved with the introduction of gas and electricity
- local authorities were providing theatres, libraries, museums, public baths and sports pitches
- newspapers carried advertisements for forthcoming attractions.

■ LEISURE IN THE TWENTIETH CENTURY

Major developments in the twentieth century include:

- the introduction of a 37-hour week
- legislation for holidays with pay (in 1938)
- vastly improved transport (air, sea and rail)
- cinema
- leisure technology in the home.

Post-war leisure   Since the 1939-45 war:

- cinema and theatre audiences have declined
- theatres, bingo halls and billiard rooms have closed
- railways have declined but the motor car reigns
- home entertainment has expanded with television, video, hi-fi and home computers becoming relatively common
- the car has made family excursions a regular occurrence
- competitive sport in schools is in decline

- participation in adult team games has declined
- action sports with only a few players have become increasingly popular.

In the twentieth century, the amount of time available for leisure, the amount of money spent on leisure and the range of activities and facilities available is greater than at any other time. The West has become a leisure-orientated society.

Conclusion

Leisure in the twentieth century has its beginnings in ancient times, although the information we have is, understandably, rather sketchy. From the point of view of sport and physical recreation, it could be argued that little has changed since those times: the highly competitive and honourable elements of track and field events remain and are reflected in the fact that the Olympic Games are important to most people.

Throughout history, leisure has been very strongly influenced by religion and many activities can trace their origins to religious festivals. Activities that today might be considered to directly conflict with the church – providing people with *alternatives* to worship – were originated either as part of religious ceremonies or by churchmen in order to attract people *to* worship. This applies to various forms of art and entertainment, to many team games and to tourism. Conversely, religion has also acted as a brake on leisure, with some of the more puritan religions banning many enjoyable leisure pursuits.

Leisure has developed as a direct result of improvements in technology. Rapid and efficient transport systems have enabled people to travel far and wide and gain a greater understanding of the world. However, as technology has advanced it has also placed pressures on society. The nature and form of leisure was changed by the Industrial Revolution, for example. Industrialists demanded much more of their employees, long hours and poor housing affected workers' health and leisure activities were provided in order to improve health and productivity. Industrialised societies became very regimented and leisure activities with very formal rules were introduced.

As we approach the end of the century, leisure has become a global concept: sporting events are beamed into our homes by television satellite; sport, recreation, art and entertainment attract tourists in their thousands to cities all over the world. 'A visit to the countryside' need no longer just mean a day out from the town or city but could refer also to a trek in the Himalayas, a flight out to Ayers Rock or an African safari. All these places and many others can be 'visited', too, by watching television. Consequently, leisure is still largely a home-based activity, but, because of its diversity and popularity, has become one of the largest and most profitable industries in the world.

Assignments

1 Produce a timetable of your own leisure activities and compare it with that of a colleague. What factors affect your leisure choices?

2 Write an article for your college magazine about the history of a major local leisure provider. Consider how the history of your chosen facility reflects the general history of the leisure industry.

3 Produce a radio report on how leisure patterns have changed during the past 50 years. For this you will need to undertake research in your local library and interview a number of senior citizens (you will find their reminiscences fascinating and well worth recording).

CHAPTER 2

LEISURE ORGANISATION

OBJECTIVES

On completion of this chapter, students will be able to:

▶ understand the classification of leisure as a service industry

▶ be aware of the various commercial structures within the industry

▶ differentiate between the private, public and voluntary sectors of the industry

▶ describe the roles and responsibilities of leisure providers.

Leisure as an industry

■ WHAT KIND OF INDUSTRY IS IT?

Industry as a whole is divided into three sectors:

- *primary* – this sector is responsible for the extraction of raw materials and includes farming, fishing and mining

- *secondary* – this is the *manufacturing* sector, which includes the car industry, textiles, chemicals and electronics, and those who work in the secondary sector convert the raw materials into goods or products for consumers

- *tertiary* – this is the *service* sector, which includes industries as varied as banking and insurance, hotel and catering, travel and leisure, retailing and distribution as well as central and local government. In the UK, over half of the workforce are employed in this sector, providing services to both the general public and other industries.

Let us now look in more detail at the leisure industry. Leisure, as an industry, comprises a wide range of both services and activities that include sport and physical recreation, art and entertainment, tourism and hospitality. Most leisure organisations can be classified as being a part of the tertiary sector, although some, for example manufacturers of leisure clothing, may be more readily classified as being part of the secondary sector. A few, such as garden centres, can be classified as being in both the primary *and* the tertiary sectors as the plants and shrubs are grown in nurseries and then sold to leisure gardeners.

Sectors of the leisure industry

In the same way that industry may be subdivided, the leisure industry can itself be divided into three sectors:

- the voluntary sector
- the public sector
- the private sector.

■ THE VOLUNTARY SECTOR

Human beings are social creatures who generally prefer to live and work in groups than on their own. The groups that we join are either *formal* or *informal*. Every group has some purpose or *objective* and a *structure*. Most have some degree of *leadership* and a system for making *decisions*. The objectives of a formal group are likely to be written down, whereas those of an informal group will be assumed.

The first informal group to which we belong is the family. It is possible, although unusual, to write down a set of objectives for a family and we can easily identify its leaders, outline its structure and describe how decisions are made within it.

Our social life is dominated by informal groups, which consist mainly of friends or acquaintances. Friendship groups are formed as a result of people having a common interest or identity. For children this will be linked to aspects of everyday life, such as their extended family, the area in which they live, school and hobbies, whereas for adults, while the childhood friendships may continue, they join other groups based on work, local leisure facilities and interests that have developed over the years.

The extent of involvement on the part of any person within a group and the range of activities that is undertaken varies considerably. It will depend on a number of factors, such as mobility, income, motivation and aptitude. Like the family, it is unusual to find written objectives for a friendship group. Also, there may not be a leader appointed within the group, although frequently one will emerge and be identified as the group member who makes decisions.

As our range of interest expands, the number of groups or organisations to which we belong generally increases. The groups themselves become increasingly formal in their structure, even if the group activities are informal. You and your friends may belong to local clubs and societies that produce a set of rules for all members. It will be a condition of membership that you agree to abide by the club rules. Once written rules are produced, there has to be someone appointed to make sure that they are applied. This gives the organisation the basis of a formal structure.

Generally, the more formal an organisation is, the more structured it becomes and the members of a club will appoint officers or officials to make sure that it is run efficiently. Usually this will be carried out through a *committee structure*, whereby club members volunteer their services to carry out management tasks within the club. Most sports clubs appoint a *committee* to manage its affairs, which will consist of a chairperson, treasurer and secretary, and may also include a match secretary, team captains, a social secretary and co-opted members (who are appointed because of their particular interests or skills). Similar committee structures exist within other leisure organisations, such as youth clubs and drama societies.

The committee is elected by the club members. Those who agree to serve on the committee become *accountable* to the members for the running of the club. The committee will meet on a regular basis to review the club's activities and ensure that it is meeting its *objectives,* that is to say, carrying out the policies agreed by the members. The committee demonstrates its accountability by producing reports of the club's activities and keeping a set of accounts that will be presented to club members for approval at an Annual General Meeting.

The objective of most clubs, associations and societies is to provide facilities and opportunities for members to participate in their chosen leisure activities. They are not necessarily run to make a profit. Their income is derived from the subscriptions paid by members, fees for use

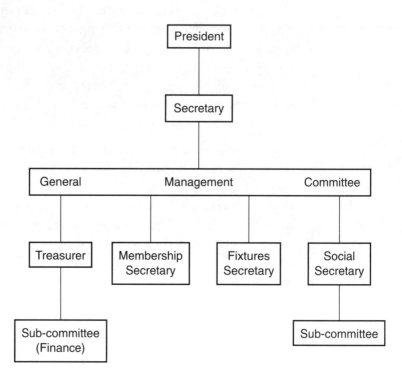

Figure 2.1
Committee
structure of a club

of the clubs' facilities and from commercial activities, such as catering and selling equipment. If the club is fortunate enough to make a profit, it will re-invest the income to improve the club's facilities.

Many of these organisations are run on a very low budget and can only survive by staging additional fund-raising activities and seeking financial help from national government, local government, charitable foundations or commercial sponsorship. The club officials are unpaid and give up large amounts of their leisure time to ensure that their organisation meets its objectives. It is because these members volunteer their services that this sector of the leisure industry is called *the voluntary sector*.

The clubs and organisations that make up the voluntary sector set objectives aimed at meeting the needs and interests of their members and users. The voluntary sector provides a backbone of opportunities for leisure for everyone in the community. In addition to providing recreational facilities, the voluntary sector gives people the opportunity to become involved in the activities of their community. It is often as a result of serving on club committees in the voluntary sector that people decide to seek a career in the leisure industry.

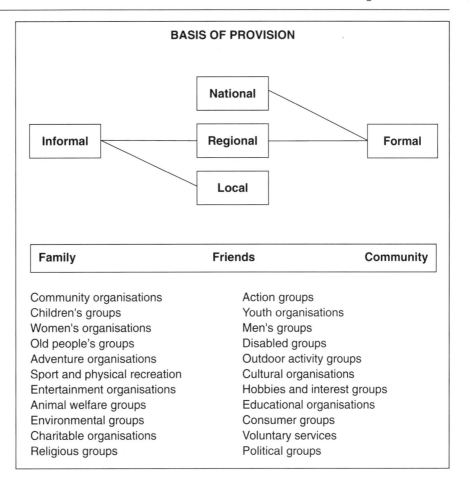

Figure 2.2
The range of structures in the voluntary sector

BASIS OF PROVISION

National

Informal — Regional — Formal

Local

| Family | Friends | Community |

Community organisations
Children's groups
Women's organisations
Old people's groups
Adventure organisations
Sport and physical recreation
Entertainment organisations
Animal welfare groups
Environmental groups
Charitable organisations
Religious groups

Action groups
Youth organisations
Men's groups
Disabled groups
Outdoor activity groups
Cultural organisations
Hobbies and interest groups
Educational organisations
Consumer groups
Voluntary services
Political groups

■ THE PUBLIC SECTOR

It would not be possible for *all* the leisure needs of a community to be provided by the voluntary sector alone. We have already seen that many clubs and societies constantly struggle for survival and have to seek assistance from other sources, including government – that is, from the public sector, which consists of national and local government.

National government

National government is seldom directly involved in the provision of leisure facilities in the UK. However, through a number of government-sponsored organisations, it provides grants to local authorities and voluntary organisations (see Figure 2.3). The principal organisations that provide funding for leisure are:

- The Arts Council
- The Sports Council
- English Heritage
- The Countryside Commission
- The Forestry Commission
- British Tourist Authority
- The Nature Conservancy Council.

In addition to this funding, local authorities receive a *rate support grant*, some of which will be channelled into leisure provision.

Figure 2.3
Government
departments that
provide funding
for leisure

Local government

Most of the facilities that local authorities provide are either those which are suitable for mass or public recreation or those that cannot be provided by the voluntary sector because of high land and building costs. Local authorities have a legal *duty* to provide some leisure amenities, such as education and libraries, although generally leisure is a *discretionary* provision. Local authorities have the power to provide for leisure, but they are not obliged to. The responsibilities of the local authority to provide community leisure facilities may be classified under the following headings:

- outdoor sport and physical recreation
- indoor sport and physical recreation
- outdoor public recreation
- cultural recreation
- education-related recreation
- tourism, conservation and heritage
- entertainment
- library and information services.

The following are often, although not always, financed by the public sector:

- museums, galleries and theatres
- swimming pools and leisure centres
- youth and community centres
- parks and open spaces
- playing fields and sports centres
- public halls and conference centres
- adult and continuing education.

Within these facilities there are likely to be bars and restaurants that will be run either by the council or contracted to independent caterers.

In order to be able to provide such a wide range of activities, the local authority has to have an *organisational structure*, a *leisure policy* and an *income*.

Figure 2.4 The British Library Round Reading Room (Courtesy of the British Library)

Structure in the public sector

The public sector, at local level, consists of the following:

- county councils
- county district councils
- parish and community councils
- in London only, London Borough Councils and
- the City Corporation.

The structures of local authority departments vary considerably, depending on whether or not they are servicing urban or rural communities as well as other factors, such as, the amenities they wish to provide, how many people they serve and how much money they wish to allocate to community leisure. It will also be strongly influenced by the political ideals of the council members.

Provision will depend on the needs of the community. A seaside resort may not need a large leisure pool, but it will need to provide a theatre to entertain visitors during the summer season. A large city may need to provide several pools, but not need to provide public entertainment because the resident population is large enough to support such facilities run by the private sector on a commercial basis. Some towns have large elderly populations and need to provide community centres, while others have large populations of families with young children and so need to provide leisure facilities for the under fives. In a rural community, the provision of parks and open spaces will not be as pressing as it would be in an inner city area.

There are two main structures that apply to the management of local authorities:

- committee structure
- departmental structure.

The committee structure

Councillors are elected by the public (the electorate) to serve on the council for three years. The councillors elect a mayor who will hold office for one year. The mayor appoints councillors to serve on committees. The committees decide on policy (objectives) and set budgets.

The departmental structure

The council appoints officers to run their facilities. Among the officers appointed, there will be a chief executive who is responsible for the departmental structure. Each department is divided into sections and the majority of council employees (officers) are employed within the sections.

The decision making process

The council is elected by the public based on its policies and previous performance. The council draws up a budget based on the costs involved in implementing its policies and this will be reviewed annually.

Each committee is allocated a budget based on the priorities agreed by full council. The committee allocates funds to its departments to implement policy and meets on a regular basis to review the performance of the departments. Each department makes recommendations to the committee regarding improvements to its services and submits estimates of the costs of running them.

The committee process is lengthy. Decisions taken in committee about funding affect future policy. Policies are adopted taking finance, the needs of the community and political factors into consideration. It is a balancing act that is aimed at satisfying as many of the electorate as possible. If the electorate are not satisfied with the performance of the council, it is able to show its disapproval by means of the electoral system.

The role of the councillor

Councillors volunteer their services to the community and are elected as representatives of the people who live in their area. They are not salaried. Councillors serving on a leisure committee are responsible for taking decisions relating to a wide range of community amenities and their duty is to ensure that there are sufficient leisure resources, facilities and recreational programmes to meet the needs of the community.

The role of a councillor on a leisure services committee is to establish policies and set objectives, to make decisions to implement and achieve them and to monitor progress. This must be done in accordance with guidelines that are set by national government and within very strict budgets.

Public-sector funding

The public sector is a business organisation and receives its income in two ways:

- capital
- revenue.

Capital income   This takes the following forms:

- direct grants and loans from central government
- loans from commercial organisations
- lotteries
- local taxes.

Capital is used to develop and construct facilities to be used by the public.

Revenue income   This takes the following forms:

- receipts from trading
- grants from central government
- local taxes.

Revenue is used to finance the day-to-day running of the facilities.

■ THE PRIVATE SECTOR

Private-sector leisure is provided by individuals or companies and is paid for by the public out of their disposable income. Commercial organisations make a major contribution to leisure and recreation provision in this country. Their range of operation is extensive and operates mainly in the secondary and tertiary levels of industry.

Here is a list of just a few of the leisure facilities that are usually provided by the private sector:

- squash courts and private leisure centres
- cinemas, bingo halls and theatres
- hotels and restaurants
- pubs and wine bars
- leisure goods and sporting equipment
- theme parks and stately homes
- travel agencies and tour operators
- home-based leisure.

The companies that are involved in the leisure industry are numerous and range from the very small sole trader to multinational companies. Unlike the public and voluntary sectors, the private sector exists with the primary objective of making a profit out of leisure.

Structure in the private sector

The sole trader

It is unusual to find sole traders involved in the direct provision of large-scale leisure as they are commonly involved in business where only small amounts of money are required. Sole traders own their business. If the business is unsuccessful, they are personally liable for any debts. Sole traders are most likely to be involved in the leisure industry in the provision of direct labour services, such as building, plumbing and maintenance. However, more and more people are providing personal, or, *ancillary services*, such as fitness counselling, catering and guide services.

Advantages of being a sole trader are that the owner:

- maintains personal control of the business
- enjoys all profits
- can take business decisions quickly
- has personal contact with staff and customers
- has confidentiality (accounts do not have to be published).

Disadvantages in being a sole trader are that:

- the owner is liable for any business debts
- raising capital may be difficult
- success depends on the owner's health and business acumen
- the business dies with the owner.

The partnership

One of the major disadvantages of a business that is run by a sole trader is that it may be difficult to raise capital. To overcome this problem a partnership may be formed.

A partnership consists of between 2 and 20 people in business together. Each partner contributes capital to the business and any profits (or losses) are shared. Decisions that one partner makes are legally binding on the other partners. It is therefore wise to choose business partners very carefully.

Although it is not a legal requirement, most partnerships are formalised by signing a *partnership agreement*. This will include details of the amount of capital contributed to the business by each partner, an agreement on how profits and losses will be shared and details of any salaries the partners may receive.

Partnerships are frequently formed by professional people who provide consultancy services, such as accountancy, legal and medical advice to the industry.

Advantages of partnerships are that there are:

- additional sources of finance
- shared responsibilities and risks
- opportunities to specialise.

Disadvantages of partnerships are that:

- all partners share unlimited liability
- profits must be shared
- decisions take longer to make and implement.

Limited companies

The majority of commercial leisure organisations are run by limited companies. There are two types of limited company:

- *private limited companies*, which are identified by the abbreviation 'Ltd' after their names
- *public limited companies*, which are much larger and are identified by the letters 'PLC' after their names.

The term 'Limited' means that the company has *limited liability*. The main advantage to becoming a limited company is that investors in the company risk only the amount of money that has been invested if the company falls into debt. People who invest their capital in a limited company are *shareholders*. They need not take part in the decision making process but appoint a *board of directors* to act on their behalf.

The majority of private limited companies are small, many of them being family businesses or sole traders or partnerships that have achieved enough success to merit expansion.

Public limited companies are usually large organisations employing hundreds or more people. Investors are able to purchase shares on the stock market. Public companies frequently consist of a *parent company*, other companies within the group being *subsidiaries*.

Public limited companies in the leisure industry are frequently household names, such as:

- Ladbrokes
- Grand Metropolitan
- Trusthouse Forte
- Granada
- Charringtons
- Virgin.

Other large companies are subsidiaries of parent companies, such as:

- Texas Homecare is a subsidiary of Ladbrokes
- Beefeater Restaurants are a subsidiary of Charringtons
- Chessington World of Adventure is a subsidiary of the Tussaud Group, which is a subsidiary of the Pearson group of companies.

The leisure industry is not just composed of household names, however, and the majority of companies that make up the private sector are private limited companies.

Advantages of limited companies are that:

- there is less risk for investors
- there are greater opportunities for expansion
- business is unaffected by illness or death of the shareholders.

Disadvantages of limited companies are that:

- there is less confidentiality (it is a legal requirement to publish annual financial reports)
- there is the possibility of conflict between directors and shareholders
- it is often impersonal.

Conclusion

The leisure industry forms a major part of the service industry. It has a complicated structure that spreads across the private, public and voluntary sectors of the industry. Further, each sector has its own, almost unique structure.

The way in which decisions are made within all organisations depends on the structure of the organisation concerned and this is as true in the leisure industry as anywhere else. This decision-making process varies considerably: an immediate response to a situation may be offered by a sole trader, but on the public sector, even a simple decision may require an extended process of consultation through a number of committees.

The provision of leisure may be based on commercial factors where leisure is to be a source of income and profit. On the other hand, it can also be non-profit making, catering for the leisure wants of a local community through clubs and societies or provided as a statutory obligation by local authorities.

The quality and quantity of leisure provision in the UK varies considerably. In rural areas, the majority of leisure is likely to be provided by the public and voluntary sectors, whereas in large towns or cities, the contribution from the private sector is much greater.

Assignments

1   Newtown Cricket and Hockey Club.

The following are officers of the Newtown Cricket and Hockey Club:

Edward Adams, Membership Secretary
Carol Burton, Captain, Ladies Hockey
Debbie Creighton, Treasurer
Mike Devereux, Captain, Men's Cricket
Michelle Edwards, Club President
Clive Fashanu, Social Section
Molly Grey, Committee Member
Ray Hall, Fixtures Secretary
Ian Isherwood, Captain Men's Hockey
Megan Jones, Captain, Ladies' Cricket
Seema Kaur, Committee Member
Vernon Lawrence, Secretary.

Prepare an organisation chart showing the structure of the committee, adding any additional officers which may be appropriate.

2   Is your local council committed to community leisure or is leisure provision mainly in the hands of the voluntary and private sector? Prepare a list of the major leisure amenities in your area, categorise them as being in the voluntary, public or private sector. Also, locate and colour code local leisure facilities on a town map. Arrange an interview with a local councillor who serves on a leisure services committee, and produce a report on their work.

3 You are a member of the management committee of a local voluntary organisation that is likely to lose money in the next financial year. You have agreed to prepare a discussion document for the committee considering strategies for increasing income. Club membership fees are already high and several members have said that they would resign if they were increased.

Prepare a list of organisations that you would approach for help, either for grants, loans or sponsorship. Also prepare a list of ways in which revenue might be increased.

CHAPTER 3

COMMUNICATION IN THE LEISURE INDUSTRY

OBJECTIVES

On completion of this chapter, students will:

▶ be aware of the difference between formal and informal communication and identify situations when their respective uses are appropriate

▶ understand and apply standard formal communication practices

▶ recognise the need for formal and informal communication within the leisure industry (The assignments at the end of the chapter give students an opportunity to apply formal and informal communication in a leisure setting)

▶ identify situations where non-verbal communication occurs.

One of the most important aspects of the leisure industry is *communication.* Of all the service industries, leisure stands out as being the most involved with *people.* In the leisure environment, communication between people – whether they are work colleagues or customers – must be *effective.* Many problems in the industry stem from misunderstanding, caused by a breakdown in the communication process. Such problems can be prevented or kept to a minimum by improving the communication skills of *everybody* employed in the industry.

Forms of communication

Communication is the process of passing instructions or information from one person or group to another. This may be:

- *one-way* or *two-way*
- *formal* or *informal*
- *verbal* or *non-verbal*.

■ ONE-WAY AND TWO-WAY COMMUNICATION

The one-way communication process has three components:

1 a sender or *transmitter*

2 a method or *medium* of transmission

3 a *receiver.*

The disadvantage of one-way communication is that the sender has no means of knowing whether or not the message sent has been received and understood.

When communication is a two-way process, however, a fourth component is involved: *feedback*

The advantage of two-way communication is that the sender is able to tell if the message has been received and understood.

■ FORMAL AND INFORMAL COMMUNICATION

Formal communication may be *written* or *verbal*. It is used in the workplace in order to establish and maintain codes of conduct and standards of practice. It is also used as a method of standardising and, hopefully, simplifying the flow of information between people at work and between a business and its customers.

The most commonly used media for formal written communication are:

- *memorandums* for issuing instructions, recording facts and making suggestions
- *reports* to convey information, report findings and put forward ideas or suggestions
- *agendas* to record items for discussion at a formal meeting
- *minutes* for recording discussions of formal meetings

- *business letters*
- *business forms.*

Formal verbal communication usually occurs in the following contexts:

- *business meetings*
- *interviews*
- *conferences*
- *presentations*
- *disciplinary hearings.*

When formal verbal communication is used, the speaker may read from a script, use notes or rehearse what is to be said beforehand. It is wise to do this to ensure that misunderstandings do not occur, especially as the occasions on which this form of communication is used are usually important.

Informal communication, on the other hand, occurs between people when they are operating in more relaxed situations. Its form depends on where and when the communication takes place and may be verbal or non-verbal.

At work, informal communication is a means of passing information between workers without the need for formal instructions. It can be inaccurate, fed by rumour and gossip, but more usually it is just a common means of interchange between colleagues. It involves a free-flowing exchange of information, recounting events and experiences or conveying information that is of mutual interest or benefit. It is usually not recorded.

One unusual feature of the leisure industry is that, behind the scenes, businesses are run on formal, even strict, lines, but the relationships with customers have to be seen to be informal:

- staff dress informally in their own clothes or are required to wear informal uniforms, such as tracksuits
- forenames are used when speaking to colleagues in the presence of customers
- identity badges emphasise forenames.

Such informal behaviour is allowed and encouraged because the customers themselves are using their leisure time for informal recreation and do not want their enjoyment restrained by formality.

■ VERBAL AND NON-VERBAL COMMUNICATION

Communication does not just involve spoken and written words: we also use our eyes, ears, hands and facial expressions to emphasise information when it is sent and to confirm the information when it is received. It is important to develop listening and observation skills and always to be aware of the extent to which our other senses are used to communicate.

Body language

From looking at the expression on someone's face we are able to tell whether they are happy, sad, bored, angry or in pain without that person saying a word. In two-way communication, the way in which we communicate is influenced by the *body language* that has been used by the correspondent.

People are often unaware of their body language, so if they try to hide their true feelings by saying the opposite of what they feel, their body language may give the game away.

Hands can be highly expressive and we use them to emphasise what we are saying. For instance, the way a person shakes hands may leave a lasting impression of their character and folded arms indicate that someone is feeling ill at ease, wishing to hide themselves.

Body language can also be misleading:

- a smile can be an expression of friendship *or* a sign of self-satisfaction
- crying can be a sign of joy *or* of grief.

When we meet someone for the first time, we will receive an impression of that person based on what we see, what we hear and what we feel.

This idea of what a person is like, formed in those few seconds in which introductions are made, will probably last a long time. It is therefore important that the communicator makes sure that the impression created is the right one.

Corporate image

The need to make a good impression is one of the reasons companies create a *corporate image* for themselves that is instantly recognised. Generally the starting point is a trademark, or, *logo* on business stationery. This is extended – staff wear it on their uniforms, it appears in the decor of their premises and is displayed on all their products. On seeing the logo, customers will identify it with a common standard of service and quality of product and expect this whenever they make use of the company's facilities.

Presentation of data

Decision making is based on the evaluation of available information. In industry, a great deal of information is presented in the form of statistics. In order to make decisions objectively, it is important that statistical information is presented in a simple and effective manner so that it can be readily absorbed and understood. The most commonly used methods of presenting data of this nature are:

- *tables* to illustrate numerical characteristics
- *graphs* to provide a visual impression of changes in one or more variables over a period of time
- *bar charts* to compare different categories by presenting them in columns of different height or length
- *pie charts* to break down a total figure into its components
- *pictograms* to show changes in variables by means of pictures
- *cartograms* to show regional, national or international patterns.

It is important to try to present your information accurately and to select a format that is appropriate to your audience. Whatever method you choose, your illustrations should:

- have a *title*
- show the *source* of information (if not original)
- be clearly *labelled*
- be *clear* and *concise.*

Conclusion

People who are employed in the leisure industry need to be accomplished practitioners of both formal and informal communication.

Although communication is usually a two-way process, those who work in the leisure environment need to be able to recognise situations where one-way communication is appropriate (such as when giving instructions). It is extremely important, however, to be able to recognise when such instructions may not have been understood (for example, when this is clear from a customer's body language).

The leisure industry consists of a vast number of different organisations, the majority of which requiring that their staff use formal, written communication. Formal communication in business is extremely important. The standardised formats of formal, written communication have developed to ensure that breakdowns in communication are kept to a minimum, so they should be learned and followed.

Assignments

You are to set up a leisure organisation with a group of colleagues.

■ TASK 1

1 Design a logo for your company.

2 List the aims and objectives that reflect the type of company you wish to form.

3 Produce a range of business documents for the company using the logo you have chosen.

■ TASK 2

You are employed as an assistant to the Manager of a leisure centre. Following several complaints from users of the leisure centre who are non-smokers, the management are considering the introduction of a smoking ban throughout the leisure centre. You have been asked to produce a report for discussion at the next board meeting.

1 Write a memorandum to all staff asking for their comments on the proposal that a smoking ban should be introduced.

2 Prepare a report and recommendations for the Board of Directors in which you consider the reasons for introducing a smoking ban. (For this, you will need to carry out research on passive smoking and provide statistical information, presenting it in a format that will be easily understood, using appropriate charts or diagrams. Conduct a smoking survey at your local leisure centre or in your college and use the results in your report.)

■ **TASK 3**

1   Prepare an agenda for a meeting of the Board of Directors to include an item discussing the smoking ban.
2   Make a verbal presentation of your findings to the Board using appropriate illustrations.

3   Produce a written report for the Board's consideration.

4   Acting as members of the Board, discuss the proposition that a smoking ban should be introduced, making notes on the discussion.

5   Prepare a set of minutes recording the verbal presentation, receipt of the written report, the debate that followed and the decision of the directors.

■ **TASK 4**

Using letterheads that you have designed, write a business letter to a firm of signwriters requesting information on the cost of no smoking signs.

■ **TASK 5**

Produce a range of signs for use in the leisure centre to encourage leisure centre users and staff not to smoke.

■ **TASK 6**

Roleplay

You are working in the leisure centre and have spotted a customer smoking in a no smoking area. How would you ask them to stop smoking if the customer is:

(a)   a personal friend
(b)   a personal friend of the Managing Director
(c)   a foreigner who speaks no English
(d)   a senior citizen
(e)   the leader of a gang, all of whom are smoking.

CHAPTER 4

FINANCE

OBJECTIVES

On completion of this chapter, students will:

▶ understand the concept of budgeting and its applications, from personal finance to financial management of a leisure facility

▶ recognise the differences between capital and revenue when applied to income and expenditure

▶ be aware of the role of national and local government in the financing of public-sector leisure

▶ be able to identify sources of financial assistance available to voluntary and private-sector leisure organisations

▶ appreciate the differences in the financial objectives of the public, voluntary and private sectors of the industry.

What is finance?

There are two commonly used definitions of *finance:*

- the management of money
- money provided by a bank or similar organisation to help run a business or buy something.

Like all businesses, those that operate in the leisure sector have a duty to ensure that they generate sufficient income to enable them to carry out their activities on a cost-recovery or profit-making basis. The golden rule, therefore, is that the organisation should not lose money. This applies to any leisure organisation, whether it is a club, a charitable body, a local authority provision, sole trader or a multinational company. This means that there has to be a process of monitoring the organisation's income and expenditure.

Finance involves taking economic decisions regarding the organisation and monitoring and evaluating the results of those decisions in the long, medium and short term. This process is the responsibility of the finance officers of the organisation concerned, although a general duty is placed on all employees or club members to be aware of the need to maximise income, minimise costs and work together to achieve the financial goals.

The purpose of finance

Business organisations have to balance their books and financial measures are taken in the following areas:

- to raise finance to allow current activities to take place and ensure that facilities and equipment are maintained
- to assist short-term planning, particularly making sure that there are sufficient monies to meet current, short-term expenditure
- to facilitate the introduction of major capital projects
- to assist long-term planning.

Budgets

All organisations operate according to a *budget* that is drawn up by examining expenditure over a period of time, usually a year. Expenditure is of two types: *revenue expenditure*, which is how much is spent on a day-to-day basis, and *capital expenditure*, which is the amount of money spent on major projects. Taken together, capital and revenue expenditure are *total expenditure*.

Personal finance

Everyone is different. A pen picture of a typical 16-year-old student would be of someone who is single, living with a family and spending their leisure time with other students who share common interests. A student may have a part-time job or be given an allowance that is spent on clothes, entertainment, sport, holidays and hobbies. Indeed, the proportion of money spent on leisure is likely to be high.

What is spent on a day-to-day basis is current or revenue expenditure. What is saved is capital.

Just suppose that you have set your heart on getting some luxury, such as a CD system, a holiday abroad or a car. It is likely that you will pay for luxuries out of your savings. What you pay for them is, therefore, capital expenditure.

Now, what happens if you cannot afford to buy these things but are absolutely desperate to have them? There are several solutions to this problem:

- you save until you have enough capital to buy them
- you ask someone you know to give you the money
- you ask someone you know to lend you the money
- you borrow the money from a bank or other financial institution.

Congratulations – you have just entered the world of finance!

You will soon find out that borrowing, whether it is through loans, on credit cards or accounts, seldom comes cheaply.

■ WHERE DOES YOUR MONEY GO?

Let us now suppose that you have a full-time job.

The amount of money you *earn* and the amount of money you *receive* are different. This is because a proportion of your income is deducted by your employer to pay your Income Tax and National Insurance.

Your *gross* pay is what you earn *before* tax, while *net* pay is what you receive *after* tax.

Income Tax is collected by the Government to fund its expenditure.

National Insurance is also collected by the Government and funds the Department of Social Security.

The money you have left after deductions, as we have seen, is your net income. In order to make sure that you can live comfortably throughout the year on your income, it is important to maintain a personal budget so that you can afford to pay for luxuries without having to borrow at high interest rates.

In addition to buying food and paying for accommodation, you will be liable to pay local taxes (Council Tax) and *Value Added Tax* (VAT, a sales tax collected by the Customs and Excise Department on behalf of central government), which is levied on the sale of most goods and services.

Public-sector finance

■ NATIONAL GOVERNMENT FINANCE

National government derives its income from taxation of individuals and businesses. Its major sources of income are:

- Income Tax
- VAT
- Corporation Tax
- death duties.

All these monies are paid into the *Treasury*. Each government department is allocated a share of the income by the Treasury. The amounts allocated and any changes in the amounts or forms of taxation are announced by the Chancellor of the Exchequer when the annual Budget is presented. (The financial year runs from April to March).

Through various statutory agencies, central government provides partial funding for capital projects undertaken by local authorities.

■ LOCAL AUTHORITY FINANCE

The local authority receives income from four areas:

- government grants
- Uniform Business Rates (UBR)
- Council Tax
- fees and charges.

Government grants

Finance from central government is usually provided via statutory government agencies such as the *Sports Council* and the *Arts Council*. If a local authority is considering building new facilities or improving existing ones, it may apply to the statutory agencies for financial assistance.

The Government will apply strict criteria in deciding whether or not to provide financial help to the local authorities asking for it. In recent years, for example, the main criteria applied are that the facilities should be able to be used all year round and be accessible to as many people as possible, particularly those who may be considered to be disadvantaged in some way.

Generally speaking, finance made available to local authorities by central government is to assist with capital expenditure and is provided in the form of a grant or loan.

Uniform Business Rates (UBR)

Local authorities receive income from commercial organisations in the form of a tax called the Uniform Business Rate. These are monies which are collected by the local authority, paid into a national pool and redistributed to each local authority in equal amounts.

Council Tax

The Council Tax replaced the unpopular Community Charge and the amount paid is based on the value of property as assessed by the Inland Revenue. Properties fall into one of eight bands. It is a local tax and is paid directly to the local authority.

The majority of a local authority's services are funded wholly or in part by the income generated by the Council Tax.

Fees and charges

The local authority receives additional income from admission fees to some of its facilities (such as leisure centres, art galleries, museums and theatres), from car parking charges, library fines and so on. This income is known as revenue income.

All local authorities have to provide funding in many areas, including education, housing, social services, planning and engineering, as well as leisure services. Each department will be allocated a budget based on the priorities, aims and objectives of the local authority concerned and how much money is available during that financial year.

Voluntary-sector finance

The simplest way to examine voluntary-sector finance is to consider the financial activities of a sports club.

Many clubs and societies are granted *charitable status*. This means they are non-profit making organisations that exist to service the needs of a community. As a result of their charitable status, they will be able to derive financial benefits, such as reductions in business rates and exemption from certain forms of taxation.

Income is usually derived from the following:

- subscriptions and membership fees
- receipts from sales of food, drink and goods

- revenue from gaming machines
- match fees
- grants and loans from local authorities and other agencies
- hiring out of facilities
- sponsorship
- interest from investment.

The most common items of expenditure involved in running a club are:

- rent and rates
- fuel cost (heating, lighting and so on)
- taxes
- hire of facilities
- staff pay and National Insurance
- repairs and general maintenance
- interest and bank charges payable on loans
- insurance
- professional fees (to solicitors, accountants, consultants)
- administrative costs
- publicity costs
- membership and affiliation fees
- cleaning and laundry
- licences
- transport.

When devising a budget, key decisions need to be taken in both these areas.
Regarding income, decisions need to be made about:

- subscription rates
- profit margins
- match fees
- hire of facilities
- sources of aid from local and national government
- methods of generating additional income.

Decisions that need to be made about expenditure concern:

- rent and rates
- repairs and maintenance
- priorities for maintenance, improvements and development
- insurance
- advertising and publicity
- pay and National Insurance

Strategies need to be devised to reduce expenditure to the minimum.

Private-sector finance

The private sector of the leisure industry consists of commercial companies. If they are unable to make a profit, they will be forced to cease trading.

Financial decisions that need to be taken by the private sector are similar to those of the public and voluntary sectors. The main differences in financial operations is that the commercial sector is more likely to seek funding for capital projects from commercial money markets.

■ SOLE TRADERS

Sole traders starting up in business are, in many ways, like a student who is still living at home: they have to rely on existing capital to start up in business or loans from the commercial banks and lending institutions, which may be hard to obtain as they will have no track record to show whether or not the loan will be a risk for the lender. It is quite possible that loans will be sought from relatives, friends or business associates before help will be sought from a bank. It is important to remember that a sole trader is responsible for any business debts incurred.

■ PARTNERSHIPS

Partnership are in a slightly better position than sole traders as each partner will be able to draw on their own sources for finance. This may, again, rely on an informal system but, because the investment risks are spread, the banks and financial institutions may consider partnerships to be a better risk.

■ LIMITED COMPANIES AND CORPORATIONS

If a larger business wishes to expand but has a shortage of capital, there are several ways in which finance may be raised:

- overdrafts
- bank loans
- commercial mortgages
- share issues.

Overdrafts

These are probably the cheapest way of raising finance in the short term. Banks are often prepared to provide companies with an overdraft facility, allowing them to borrow a limited amount of money on a regular basis, to overdraw on their current account.

Overdrafts should not be used for capital spending and should be used only to solve cash flow problems where money is owed to a business but has not yet been received.

Bank loans

Bank loans should be used for medium-term finance. Most business loans are taken out for repayment over any period from three to ten years. The loans are usually secured against the assets of the company and guaranteed by the owners. Interest is charged on the loan and the repayments are made on a monthly or quarterly basis spread over the duration of the loan.

Commercial mortgages

Commercial mortgages use land, property or business assets as security against a loan. If the borrower fails to repay the loan plus any interest by an agreed date, the lender may take possession of the land, property or assets that have been mortgaged.

Sole traders, partnerships and larger private-sector organisations often use commercial mortgages as a form of finance.

Share issues

Companies sometimes have major expansion plans that are too large to be funded by loans from financial institutions. It is possible, however, to raise capital from other sources and this is often done by means of the issue of shares.

A share issue invites other people to buy a proportion of the business, each investor (shareholder) then receives a share of the profits that are made.

Raising capital in this way has some major advantages over other forms of financing:

- it increases capital, which gives the company a much sounder financial base
- banks, as a result of this, may be prepared to lend more money, recognising the confidence that the new shareholders have in the ability of the company to make profits.

Usually, shares are only issued by larger businesses.

■ GOVERNMENT HELP TO THE PRIVATE SECTOR

Many businesses have difficulty financing their operations, particularly in the early stages, because it can be hard to obtain unsecured loans. To overcome these problems, the Government operates a loan guarantee scheme for loans to small businesses. The charges for acting as guarantor are high (usually 2.5 per cent above the normal rates of interest) and such loans are only available to certain types of business. There are, however, other schemes that help business expansion either by providing tax relief to investors or the provision of direct grants.

Other areas where assistance may be available are those that are scheduled for major redevelopment. This applies mainly to inner city and rural areas where there are high levels of unemployment, declining traditional industries and major social problems arising from unemployment.

A major source of funding in recent years has been via the EC.

Conclusion

In order to ensure its survival, it is essential that any leisure organisation maintains tight control of its finances.

Most leisure organisations monitor their income and expenditure and make plans for financial management in the short, medium and long term.

Businesses derive revenue income from the services they offer to their customers and are able to invest profits in capital projects, which are usually intended to improve the range of facilities available and therefore increase the profits.

Capital projects are frequently very costly and there are many ways in which a leisure organisation may seek to obtain funding from outside sources. For the public and voluntary sectors, this is frequently achieved by means of grants or loans from national and/or local government, but, for the private sector, funding is more likely to come from the private money markets.

Assignments

1   How much do you spend on leisure? Prepare a weekly budget of your spending. What percentage of your income do you spend on leisure? What percentage of your income do you save?

2   You wish to buy a CD system for £500. Collect as many different leaflets as you can on personal loans, credit cards and accounts from your local banks, building societies and retail outlets. Then produce a chart showing the *actual* cost of borrowing from the different organisations. Write a summary report on the 'best' loans available from the commercial sector.

3   Arrange an interview with a senior officer from the leisure services department of your local authority. What capital expenditure is planned in the near future and what assistance is being sought from central government? What proportion of the Council Tax is allocated to leisure?

4   You and your colleagues are starting a small leisure business and require funding. Prepare a business plan to present to a local bank manager.

5   Obtain copies of the annual reports of three private-sector leisure organisations. Using the financial information contained in the reports, which would you be prepared to invest in? Chart any movements in their share prices over a one-month period. What factors influenced the share prices in the time that you were monitoring them? How do the prices in leisure compare with the FT All Shares Index over the time you have selected?

6   Arrange a meeting with the treasurer of a local voluntary organisation. Find out the major financial problems that face them. Then, produce a report of your interview identifying the major financial problems the organisation encounters. Form a committee to propose and consider solutions, then write a summary report of your findings to present to the treasurer for future consideration.

CHAPTER 5

SPORT AND PHYSICAL RECREATION

OBJECTIVES

On completion of this chapter, students will:

▶ be aware of the developments that have taken place in the sport and recreation industry in the past 25 years and be able to explain why some activities have declined in popularity

▶ identify the Government's national agencies that contribute to the funding of sport and physical recreation in the UK and outline the financial mechanisms used to achieve their objectives

▶ outline the role of local authorities and their statutory obligations in providing sporting and recreational facilities and explain how such activities are funded

▶ appreciate the contribution that is made to sport and recreation by the voluntary sector and identify sources of funding for their activities

▶ recognise those aspects of the industry that are managed by the private sector and account for their involvement

▶ understand the importance of commercial sponsorship of spectator sports and explain the benefit that sponsors derive from their activities

The heading 'Sport and physical recreation' covers a wide range of activities and pastimes that are undertaken by groups or individuals during their leisure time. Historically, sport and physical recreation were activities that took place when work had finished for the day. Most sporting activities were physical and aimed at improving the survival and military skills of those who took part. Industrialisation and urbanisation created different leisure needs and wants that were provided either by the public sector or the church. From these beginnings, a pattern and structure for the provision of sport and physical recreation evolved that centred mainly on a concern for the physical health of employees or the spiritual well-being of parishioners.

In the last 25 years, there has been a major change in the pattern and range of provision of sporting and physical recreation facilities in this country. People have more time and money to spend on sport and physical recreation and local authorities are increasingly expected to provide modern, family leisure facilities. Much of this increased demand has been generated by the media and advertising. Pools with water slides and wave machines and leisure centres with full catering facilities are replacing public baths and sports halls. The importance of the team game on a Saturday afternoon has been replaced with demands for all-weather (indoor) facilities that can be used during the week as well as at weekends. In fact, it is becoming increasingly difficult to differentiate between physical recreation and entertainment – keep fit classes have become aerobics sessions, fashion designers have teamed up with sportswear manufacturers and snooker and pool halls, squash courts and fitness clubs are common facilities in most towns.

KEY FACTS ABOUT SPORT IN SOCIETY

- In Britain, $21^1/_2$ million adults and 7 million children take part in sport or exercise at least once a month.

- The most popular form of physical recreation is walking.

- Of children, 50 per cent give up sport when they finish their education.

- Recreational and cultural activities provide employment for more than 375 000 people.

- Households in the UK spend more than 15 per cent of their total expenditure on leisure-based items.

- British industry sponsors sport to the tune of £200m per year.

- Central Government invests over £500m in sport and recreation.

- The Government receives more than $£2^1/_2$ billion from sport in Income Tax, VAT and excise duties.

Sport and the Government

Leisure is one of the fastest growing industries in the UK. Sport and physical recreation form a substantial part of the leisure industry and their economic and social importance have long been acknowledged by Government. The Government is not a direct provider of sporting and recreational facilities but, through a number of statutory agencies, as we have seen briefly earlier, it is an important *enabler* and provides loans, grants and technical assistance to local authorities. Responsibility for sport and physical recreation at Government level rests with the Department of National Heritage and its Minister for Sport.

■ THE STATUTORY AGENCIES

The Sports Council

The Sports Council was established by Royal Charter in 1972 and its main objectives are:

- to increase participation in sport and physical recreation
- to increase the quality and quantity of sports facilities
- to raise standards of performance
- to provide information for and about sport.

The Sports Council is responsible for the administration of five National Sports Centres, although the management services provided at the Centres are put out to private tender. The centres and their activities are:

- Bisham Abbey – tennis, soccer, hockey, squash, weight training and golf
- Crystal Palace – athletics, swimming, boxing, martial arts, judo and basketball
- Lilleshall – soccer, table tennis, cricket, gymnastics, archery, hockey and golf
- Holme Pierrepont – water-based activities
- Plas y Brenin – mountain activities.

The Sports Council is funded by a grant from the Department of National Heritage. The Council raises additional income from commercial activities and attracts sponsorship from the private sector for specific activities.

The Sports Council provides grants and loans to local authorities for the development and provision of local community facilities and for special projects. It also makes grants to the national governing bodies of sports and associated national organisations with the specific aims of improving administration, developing participation and improving standards through coaching and training.

The Council functions through nine regional offices, which are responsible for implementing the Council's policies within those regions. The regional offices provide local authorities, voluntary sports bodies and associated organisations with advice and technical support. There are separate Sports Councils for Wales, Scotland and Northern Ireland that are funded by their respective Offices of State.

In addition to providing financial assistance to local authorities and sporting associations, the Sports Council raises public awareness of the importance of sport by means of national publicity campaigns, such as 'Sport for all'. It is particularly concerned with increasing the range of opportunities for sport and physical recreation available to low participant groups and promoting participation in sport on the part of young people, women, ethnic minorities and the disabled. In order to reduce the direct costs of such publicity campaigns, the Sports Council receives sponsorship from large private-sector organisations, such as the Midland Bank and the Milk Marketing Board, and will work in partnership with other national organisations, such as the YMCA.

Public-sector sport and recreation

In the public sector, local authorities are responsible for the provision of a range of facilities that contribute towards the sporting and recreational needs of the general public. There is considerable overlap between the public, private and voluntary sectors. As a general rule, the local authority provides or maintains the following facilities for sport or physical recreation:

outdoor sport:
- playing fields and sports pitches
- public golf courses
- bowling greens
- sports stadiums

Figure 5.1 Public amenity – playing field

Figure 5.2 Public amenity – swimming pool

indoor sport:

- swimming pools
- gymnasiums
- sports halls

- ice rinks
- leisure centres

recreation:

- play spaces
- parks and gardens
- adult education centres

- allotments
- community centres

This list is by no means exhaustive and local authorities constantly review what they provide. The range of facilities provided depends on the size of the local authority, its policies and responsibilities and other demands made on it by the community. For example, a major urban authority is more likely to provide extensive facilities whereas a rural authority, serving a relatively small and scattered community, may be unable to generate sufficient income from the Council Tax and grant funding to provide anything more than a skeleton service.

Local authorities have a statutory duty to provide public libraries, adult education and youth services. They are also permitted to provide *cultural recreation*, *non-cultural recreation* and *countryside recreation*:

- cultural recreation is museum services, theatres and arts centres
- non-cultural recreation is sports and leisure centres
- countryside recreation is parks, picnic sites and allotments.

It is through these discretionary powers that many unseen aspects of leisure provision are carried out. Councils are able to make their own facilities and equipment available for public use either free of charge or for a fee. They also have the power to make discretionary grants to voluntary organisations providing recreational facilities in the area and to enter into partnership agreements with companies in the private sector.

■ COMPULSORY COMPETITIVE TENDERING (CCT)

The Government's Compulsory Competitive Tendering legislation was passed under the 1988 Local Government Act. Since August 1993, all local authorities in England have been required to put the management of sports and leisure facilities out to private tender. The effects of this legislation are still the subject of considerable debate. It is already bringing many changes to the provision and organisation of local authorities' recreation services.

| The argument in favour of CCT | Competition for the management of sporting and leisure facilities will bring savings to local authorities and a better standard of service to the customer. |

| The argument against CCT | The legislation is weighted against the local authority's own workforce and the service offered will cost customers more and the range will be restricted to activities that are profitable. |

| What does CCT mean? | By implementing CCT, local authorities are required to invite companies from the private sector to manage sport and leisure facilities. It is possible that the most acceptable bid or tender may come from the local authority's own workforce. It is not privatisation as the local authorities still own the facilities and, by means of the committee process, retain direct control over how they are used, still deciding on pricing, programming, opening hours and quality and standards of service. |

Figure 5.3 Sports centre

The management functions that are involved are:

- taking bookings
- collection of and accounting for fees and charges
- cleaning and maintaining buildings, grounds, sports surfaces, plant and equipment
- supervising activities
- providing instruction in the sport and recreational activities offered
- catering and the provision of refreshments
- provision and hire of sports and other equipment
- paying for heating, lighting and other service charges
- securing the premises
- marketing and promotion of the facilities.

The facilities concerned are:

- sports centres
- athletics grounds
- leisure centres
- pitches for team games
- swimming pools
- cycle tracks
- golf courses and putting greens
- bowling greens and bowling centres
- centres for watersports and boating
- artificial ski slopes
- riding centres and courses for riding
- gymnasiums
- centres for flying, ballooning or parachuting
- bowling alleys
- badminton, squash and tennis courts.

Voluntary-sector sport and recreation

The voluntary sector provides many of the sport and recreational facilities in the UK. Most amateur sports clubs are run on a voluntary basis and many own their facilities although others rent their facilities from the public sector. As local sports clubs provide a service to the community, they are frequently given financial assistance by the local authority, either in the form of grants or renting pitches and other facilities at a reduced rate. The extent to which they are helped is at the discretion of the local authority.

■ THE NATIONAL PLAYING FIELDS ASSOCIATION

The National Playing Fields Association (NPFA) was founded in 1925 to encourage the provision of playing fields, playgrounds and recreation facilities on a national basis. During the period from its foundation to the present day, its role has changed significantly. Given that most local authorities now have a commitment towards the provision of both outdoor and indoor leisure facilities, which was its original purpose, it

Figure 5.4 Bowling club hall

now places emphasis on the provision of facilities for the handicapped and disabled.

As a registered charity, one of its major concerns is inevitably that of fund-raising. In addition to voluntary donations, the NPFA is partially funded by the Sports Council (£385 000 in 1988/9).

The NPFA is increasingly becoming a facilitating agency rather than a provider of leisure facilities. It offers technical advice on the provision, design, layout and construction of playing fields, provides information on sources of financial assistance and can make grants and low-interest loans for projects.

■ THE ASSOCIATION FOR CHILDREN'S PLAY AND RECREATION

The Association for Children's Play and Recreation (Playboard) was established in 1983 as a result of pressure from the NPFA. It is an organisation that was initially sponsored by the Department of the Environment with a grant of £700 000 per annum for three years. It is now a totally independent voluntary organisation.

Playboard's aims are to promote facilities for play, recreation and other leisure-time activities for children by providing advice and assistance to both the public and voluntary sectors in order to improve the quality and quantity of opportunities for children in their spare time.

Private-sector sport and recreation

The private sector is interested in providing leisure for profit. It is unusual, therefore, to find private-sector companies providing facilities for sport and physical recreation *unless* they attract the public in large numbers or involve smaller numbers who spend a lot of money. The commonest areas for private-sector involvement are:

- golf
- tennis
- water sports
- squash
- snooker and pool
- ten pin bowling

Figure 5.5 Squash lessons

- ice skating
- fitness clubs.

The common factor in all the above sports is that they require major capital investment either in land or facilities. Most private-sector organisations providing such facilities will also be involved in the sale or hire of the equipment necessary to participate in the sports concerned and, often, the provision of various kinds of catering and hospitality.

■ MULTINATIONAL PRIVATE-SECTOR COMPANIES

Due to mergers and takeovers, multinational companies dominate private-sector leisure. The range of their interest encompasses the whole of the leisure industry, but some are particularly concerned with sport and physical recreation, especially sports goods and equipment manufacturers, such as:

- Dunlop
- Nike
- Adidas
- Slazenger
- Wilson
- Head.

Other companies have major sport and physical recreation interests, but are household names for other products:

- Trusthouse Forte
- Grand Metropolitan
- Virgin
- First Leisure
- Brent Walker
- Ladbrokes
- Mecca Leisure
- Granada.

■ SPECTATOR SPORTS AND SPONSORSHIP

Spectator sports are usually run by the governing bodies of the sports concerned. However, the situation is changing in some areas, notably association football where some of the larger first-division clubs have been floated on the stock market.

The private sector are involved in spectator sports in two ways: through sponsorship and through television. Since the early 1950s, the number of spectators attending football matches has declined, but the clubs and the Football Association have been compensated by the very high fees that television companies are prepared to pay for the rights to televise matches. Other spectator sports – particularly tennis, golf and cricket – have attracted higher numbers of spectators as a result of being televised. These 'marketable' sports, in turn, attract high levels of sponsorship from the private sector.

The extent of sponsorship varies enormously. Large, multinational companies sponsor international events, teams and individual participants; smaller companies make small, but nevertheless significant contributions through the donation of prizes and advertising in programmes at smaller, local events.

Sponsorship of sport is not confined to sports and leisure companies. In fact, the major sponsors are more likely to be suppliers or producers of financial services, alcohol, tobacco, oil or confectionery. This is because sponsoring an event creates a good impression and buys respectability. Companies sponsor sport for the purposes of publicity rather than for the good of the sport itself.

Conclusion

The Government does not make a direct contribution to the provision of sporting and recreational facilities in the UK. However, through agencies such as the Sports Council it provides substantial funding for sport and recreation.

The Sports Council and other agencies provide grants and loans to all sectors of the industry. These agencies act as facilitators rather than direct providers. The Sports Council is additionally responsible for the running of centres of excellence or National Sporting Centres and provides publicity and information services on all aspects of sport and physical recreation.

Local authorities have some statutory obligations to provide sporting and recreational facilities and the extent of their provision depends greatly on the political composition of the local council. Other factors that determine the extent of provision are largely demographic (the size and age of population, the nature of the area served by the local authority – urban or rural) or may be determined by the historical importance of sport and recreation in the local community.

The management structure of local authority sports facilities is undergoing major changes through the imposition of Competitive Contract Tendering (CCT).

The voluntary sector represents the backbone of the sport and recreation industry. The governing bodies of most sports are staffed by volunteers and they are funded by annual levies on their participants. The majority of sports clubs and associations are part of the voluntary sector but they derive their income from subscriptions, assistance from local authorities, small-scale commercial activities (catering and bar services) and from sponsorship by local companies.

The commercial sector of sport and recreation is dominated by the providers of facilities used by individuals rather than team participants (such as squash clubs, golf clubs and fitness centres). The private sector invests in major capital projects. Investors require a significant return on their investment, participation in the private sector can be fairly expensive. Many private-sector organisations are multinational in their activities and have considerable leisure interests.

Although the number attending spectator sports are in decline, sports clubs are able to benefit from commercial sponsorship. Major sporting events attract a large number of sponsors who benefit from the advertising and national television coverage of the events themselves. Individual sportspeople are also able to benefit from the fees they receive for endorsing sports and leisure clothing and equipment.

Assignments

1 Using a large-scale map, produce a colour-coded profile of the major providers of sport and recreation in your area.

2 Produce a report on sport and recreation in your area, highlighting the more popular activities and detailing which sectors of the leisure industry provide them.

3 Produce a video on sport and recreational facilities in your area that are provided for the socially disadvantaged.

4 Use your video in order to seek future sponsorship from local businesses for activities featured in your film.

5 Sport is becoming increasingly commercialised. Prepare a document for discussion on the advantages and disadvantages for a professional football club of becoming a public company.

CHAPTER 6

TOURISM

OBJECTIVES

On completion of this chapter, students will:

▶ appreciate the wide range of leisure-based activities that make up the tourism product

▶ be able to outline the structure of the retail travel industry and public-sector tourism organisations

▶ recognise the contribution that tourism makes to the national economy

'Tourism is the temporary movement of people to destinations outside their normal place of work and residence, the activities undertaken during their stay in these destinations and the facilities created to cater for their needs.' (Mathieson and Wall, 1982)

Forms of tourism

People going on package holidays are travelling; day trips to the coast are excursions; overseas visitors in London are sightseeing; family outings to theme parks are recreation; the audience at the Cup Final at Wembley Stadium are spectating; Crufts Dog Show is a leisure exhibition.

All of these are forms of tourism, as are visits to stately homes and gardens, museums and art galleries, theatre trips, shopping expeditions and days out in the country, Tourism can be purely recreational, educational or a mixture of the two.

The definition tells us that tourism has three components:

- travel
- activity
- use of facilities.

Travel may be by road, rail, sea or air and tourists may use private or public transport.

Activity ranges from passive activities, such as sightseeing or attending a summer school, to highly physical, involving pursuits, such as water sports, skiing or rock climbing.

Facilities used for tourism are numerous and include hotels and restaurants, specialist services, such as guiding and tuition, and the hiring out of special equipment in order to enable tourists to participate.

Tourism may be an individual, family or group activity. Its providers are found in the public, private and voluntary sectors. What is being provided is essentially a service, although the tourist may, at various stages, purchase or use tourist products. It is usually planned in advance (in the case of holidays it is also paid for in advance). It cannot be brought to the consumer, the consumer has to be taken to the product. The tourist frequently has to rely on descriptions of the tourist attractions provided in leaflets and brochures in order to decide what to visit.

Tourism is often a component of other activities. For example, when sales representatives are on a business trip and they visit the theatre in the evening, they become tourists in their leisure time. This makes tourism quite unique as it crosses all the boundaries of leisure but is also an activity in its own right.

A particularly important aspect of tourism is that it is frequently a linking feature between the various sectors of the leisure industry. For example, an international sporting tournament is sport and recreation to the competitor, while, for the spectator, it may be both recreation *and* entertainment. Further, competitor and spectator alike will have travelled away from their work or home environment to reach the venue and can, therefore, be classified as tourists. The participants will use a number of facilities created specifically for their needs. When major events such as the Olympic Games or the World Cup take place, many other facilities are developed to cater for the large influx of visitors who attend the event. These facilities are likely to remain after the event has finished and become part of the tourism infrastructure of the city or country concerned.

Read the letter, shown opposite, written by an overseas visitor in London to relatives back home and list the different tourist services and facilities that are mentioned.

The Savoy Hotel
Strand
London

Dear Mom and Dad,

The flight from New York was great and we arrived at Gatwick Airport
yesterday morning. A porter with the quaintest cockney accent made sure we
got on the train to Victoria Station where we met our tour guide at a
special group meeting point. We went right past Buckingham Palace on the
coach from the station to the hotel and saw the Changing of the Guard. We
didn't see the Queen, she's staying at Windsor Castle.

We went shopping this morning and have taken lots of photos of the displays in
the Food Hall at Harrods. We had the film developed while we were there. After
Harrods we had a pub lunch and then took a London Bus to Madame Tussauds. The
line outside was so long! There were a couple of street entertainers. We
caught a cab back to the hotel. The cab went through Soho so we were able to
see some of the clubs that Uncle Elmer is always talking about.

We're going on a sightseeing tour of London tomorrow: The Tower of London,
and the Crown Jewels, then the British Museum and the National Gallery. On
Wednesday we head for Stratford-upon-Avon, stopping at Oxford and Blenheim
Palace where Winston Churchill was born. Warwick Castle (which is owned by
the Tussauds Group) is only a few miles away. We will be visiting
Shakespeare's birthplace and going to the theater in the evening.

After the tour we're renting a car to visit relatives in Liverpool. They tell
me they've really done a lot to the Liverpool Docks and have TV studio tours
and an art gallery there. We're going to drive into Wales and climb Mount
Snowdon.

We've decided to visit Scotland too! The travel agent next to the hotel has
suggested booking an inclusive tour. The Edinburgh Festival is on so there
should be some great entertainment. The price includes a side trip to visit
Loch Ness and search for the Monster! The receptionist in the Scottish
Tourist Office here in London says that we should be able to fit in a round
of golf at St Andrews and has given us the name of a whisky distillery and a
woollen mill to visit.

Westminster Abbey, Tea at the Ritz, 'The Mousetrap' and Hamleys toy shop
will have to wait until next year! Boy, the dollars don't go far in London
but we're having a swell time!

With love,

Dwight and Martha

Figure 6.1
Coach tour

In this letter, more than 30 different aspects of tourism are mentioned. These can be classified as being *services, products* or *activities:*

- *services* air travel, road transport (coach, bus, taxi, car, rental), travel agent, tour operator, tour guide, tourist information, banking (foreign exchange), hotels, catering (pubs and restaurants) plus other miscellaneous services (porters and receptionist)
- *products* photography, leisure shopping, crafts and souvenirs
- *activities* sightseeing, heritage attractions – castles, churches and stately homes; cultural attractions – museums and galleries; countryside – e.g. Mount Snowdon and Loch Ness; art and entertainment – theatres, nightclubs, festivals; sport and recreation – golf and others – e.g. industrial tours.

The structure of the tourism industry

Tourism is a vast industry that ranges in its scope from running a major international airline to a souvenir stall at the seaside. The key factor for tourism development is travel. Without it, the creation of sustainable business operations in the activity and facility sectors is very difficult. Therefore, when looking at the structure of the industry, travel is regarded as being the central feature.

Tourism forms just one part of the travel industry as a whole. The provision of public transport is a commercial activity. Transport operators in the public sector have to provide essential services that may, in fact, be loss-makers (this is particularly true of rail and bus transport on busy commuter networks or in rural areas). Tourism can help to offset financial losses either by supplementing the number of passengers who regularly use the loss-making routes, by increasing the numbers of passengers using them at off-peak times, or by using the profits from successful tourist routes to subsidise other loss-making operations.

Transport is a capital-intensive industry. Airlines, railways and shipping companies need to invest large amounts of money in buildings, planes, trains or ships and equipment in order to provide modern, efficient services to their customers, Governments also need to provide money to build roads and motorways for car owners and coach operators. Transport providers are able to benefit from economies of scale where the unit costs (that is, the costs per passenger) may be reduced. Tourism as an industry has evolved as a result of the economies of scale made possible by improvements in transport technology.

The retail sector of travel

■ TOUR OPERATORS

A package holiday consists of three main components:

- travel
- accommodation
- travel services (transfers, car hire, excursions and so on).

The 'package' is put together by a tour operator who negotiates contracts with *principals* (the tourism providers). By buying in bulk, well in advance of travel, the operator obtains substantial discounts from the principals. The tour operator then assembles individual packages that are sold either direct to the customer or through a travel agent. After taking a reasonable profit, any savings that are made are passed on to the customer.

The tour operator's reputation and likelihood of success is dependent on several factors:

- the quality of the product
- the service provided to clients
- the effectiveness of the brochure.

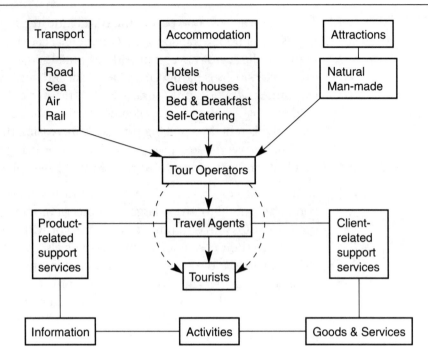

Figure 6.2
The roles of tour operators and travel agents

mention

The advantages of the inclusive or package holiday to the customer are:

- *price* economies of scale achieved by the operator are passed on to the client
- *time* the customer saves time by buying a holiday 'off the shelf'
- *convenience* the customer makes one payment for the holiday.

Tour operators come in all shapes and sizes They may be part of large multinational companies, such as Thomsons, owning some or all of the companies that provide the principal components of the holiday and offering holiday packages on a world-wide basis. On the other hand, they can be run by an individual with only a small operation, offering a product with only limited appeal to a small, specialist market.

In order to produce and sell package holidays, a tour operator carries out a number of different operational functions. When designing programmes of holiday packages, the tour operator takes the operational costs into consideration and 'builds them' into the package price.

These are some of the operational costs that a tour operator has to consider when costing a holiday programme:

- *market research* identifying potential principals and customers
- *contracts* buying products from principals

- *marketing* producing and distributing advertising and publicity material, including brochures
- *reservations* maintaining a booking system– manual or computerised
- *accounts* maintaining and monitoring financial systems within the company
- *sales* direct selling to customers and liaison with travel agents
- *resort representation* employment of company representatives or agents in destination resorts
- *personnel and office administration.*

■ TRAVEL AGENTS

A travel agent's role is to sell travel products and provide advice and information to clients.

Travel agents do not charge their customers for their service, but instead are paid commission by the companies whose products they sell.

Figure 6.3 Benidorm (Courtesy Thomsons Holidays)

Travel agents carry out a range of different activities. Some specialise in particular aspects of travel, such as long-haul or business travel, but the majority are general retail agents, selling a wide range of popular summer sun and winter sports holidays.

In recent years, the structure of retail travel in the UK has changed dramatically and the industry is dominated by multiple outlet agencies such as Thomas Cook, Hogg Robinson, Lunn Poly, AT Mays and Pickfords. There are still, however, many hundreds of small, independent agencies who, although unable to achieve the high levels of market penetration of the multiples, provide a friendly, efficient and local service that may be readily adapted to meet the needs of the communities they serve.

Regardless of the *type* of agency, there is a range of tasks that anyone working in travel must carry out in order to provide an efficient service:

- advising customers on all aspects of travel
- making reservations with principals and tour operators
- planning travel itineraries
- calculating airline, ferry, rail and coach fares
- issuing tickets, vouchers and other travel documentation
- dealing with written and telephone enquires from clients
- maintaining accurate customer files and accounts
- ordering and displaying brochure stocks
- keeping accounts
- liaising with principals and clients in the event of complaints

With advances in technology, many of these activities have become partially or totally computerised. Most counter staff, therefore, should be able to use information technology in the workplace.

The key to running an effective travel agency is to ensure that staff employed there have sufficient product knowledge and technical skills to provide impartial and professional advice to their clients. This can be a problem as the main selling tool and source of information for the travel agent is the tour operator's brochure, which is, inevitably, going to show elements of bias. The travel agent must, therefore, seek out other sources of information – guide books, tourist offices, databases and so on, participate in the educational promotions tour operators themselves provide and, most importantly, obtain client feedback.

Public-sector tourism

Tourism plays a very important part in Britain's economy. It makes a major contribution towards the balance of payments and provides and creates jobs (frequently in areas of high unemployment). Without tourism, many stately homes and museums would have to close. Other industries, such as art and entertainment, also benefit substantially from tourism.

In the UK, the Government is concerned mainly with promoting tourism rather than providing it itself. Two government organisations play a particularly important role in the promotion of tourism: The British Tourist Authority and The National Tourist Boards.

■ THE BRITISH TOURIST AUTHORITY

The British Tourist Authority (BTA) is funded by the Department of National Heritage. It is responsible for promoting tourism to Britain in overseas countries and is administered from a central office in London. It has regional offices throughout the world and employs approximately 400 people in the UK and abroad.

Its objectives are:

- to maximise the benefit to the economy of tourism to Britain from abroad while working world-wide in partnership with the private and public-sector organisations involved in the industry and the English, Scottish and Welsh Tourist Boards
- to identify the requirements of visitors to Britain, whatever their origin, and to stimulate improvements in the quality of the services and so on provided and use the best available technology to achieve them
- to ensure that the economic benefits of tourism to the UK are spread more widely and encourage this particularly in areas that have potential for tourism and higher than average levels of unemployment
- to encourage tourists to visit the UK in off-peak periods
- to advise the Government on tourism matters affecting the UK
- to ensure that the Authority makes the most cost-effective use of resources in pursuing its objectives.

The main role of the BTA is that of a tourism marketing agency. It liaises closely with tourism organisations in both the public and private sectors in order to achieve its aims.

■ THE NATIONAL TOURIST BOARDS

There are National Tourist Boards (NTBs) for England, Wales, Scotland and Northern Ireland. They were established in 1969 following the implementation of the Tourism Development Act. The English Tourist Board is a division of the Department of National Heritage, while the other Boards are the responsibility of the state departments of their respective countries.

The National Tourist Boards are responsible for encouraging the British to take holidays in Britain. The objectives of the English Tourist Board, for instance, are very similar to those of the BTA:

- to stimulate the development of English tourism by, first, encouraging the British to take holidays in England and, second, by providing and improving facilities for tourists in England

- to develop and market tourism in close co-operation with Regional and National Tourist Boards, the British Tourist Authority, local authorities and public-sector organisations as well as the private sector

- to advise government and public bodies on all matters concerning tourism in England

- to maximise tourism's contributions to the economy by creating wealth and jobs.

- to enhance the image of England as a tourism destination using all appropriate means, including undertaking and encouraging innovative marketing

- to encourage and stimulate the successful development of tourism products of a high standard that also offer good value for money

- to bring about a greater recognition of tourism as an industry for investment, employment and economic development by providing information and, where appropriate, advice and financial support

- to produce and disseminate information on tourism to the trade and consumers

- to research trends in tourism and consumer requirements to show marketing and development needs and opportunities, plus evaluate past performance, future prospects and the impact of tourism

- to improve the industry's status and performance by encouraging and stimulating the adoption of up-to-date business methods and appropriate technology as well as the provision of education and training programmes

Figure 6.4
UK Waterway
Holidays
brochure

- to ensure that England's unique character and heritage is recognised and protected through the sensitive management of its tourism.

■ REGIONAL TOURIST BOARDS

There are 12 Regional Tourist Boards in England, 3 in Wales and 32 in Scotland. They have four sources of income:

- grant funding from National Tourist Boards
- contributions from county and district councils within the areas they cover
- membership fees from tourism organisations and operators in their area
- income from other commercial activities.

In order to qualify for grant funding from the National Tourist Boards, the Regional Tourist Boards are required to set objectives and ways of measuring their performance.

The activities of the regional Boards are similar to those of the ETB and are concerned with marketing their respective regions in order to attract more British and overseas visitors to them.

■ LOCAL TOURIST OFFICES

Most towns, cities and districts that have places of interest to tourists located within them provide a local tourist information centre (TIC).

These services are funded by local authorities, supported by membership fees from other local tourism providers and enablers. They also derive an income from commercial activities.

The TIC's are extremely important to tourism in this country. They provide a link between visitors and the communities that are being visited. They provide a wide range of information on tourist attractions in their area, often provide a local accommodation service and more specialist information on specific subjects, such as access for the disabled.

Some towns and resorts provide tourist information as a part of a larger tourism department that co-ordinates the policy regarding tourism for the immediate area. Working closely with local authority leisure services departments, the tourism, marketing and development officer is responsible for promoting the area to the travel trade, to conference organisers and to visiting journalists, providing not only general publicity information of the sort required by the local TIC, but also designing or commissioning additional publicity materials, such as videos and posters to promote tourism at exhibitions and trade shows.

Conclusion

Tourism is a leisure-based activity that involves travel away from the home and work environment. In the last century, tourism has grown quite dramatically as a direct result of improvements in travel technology. Because of tourists' demands, a whole industry has been created that exists in parallel with, and as a part of, the leisure industry.

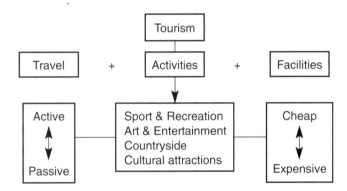

Figure 6.5
The link between tourism and leisure

Tourism comprises travel, activities undertaken while travelling or on having reached a destination and the use of facilities and services provided for the tourist. These services and activities are likely to form a part of the leisure provision for the community being visited (see Figure 6.5).

The retail travel industry has been built around the need to satisfy the demands of the travelling public and acts as the agent for many different principals, ranging from national airlines to independent travel guides.

National government recognises the importance of tourism to the economy and, through the Department of National Heritage, oversees the activities of the British Tourist Authority and National and Regional Tourist Boards who, in turn, contribute to the activities of local tourist offices and tourist information centres.

Visitor attractions are run by the public, private and voluntary sectors and there are many instances of close co-operation to be found within the industry, particularly through joint marketing initiatives. As a result of such initiatives, it can be seen that, of all leisure facility users, tourists are most likely to make use of the services provided in *all* sectors of industry.

Assignments

1 Prepare a display stand of tourist attractions in your area. In order to carry out this task successfully, it will be necessary to obtain information from your local tourist information centre and from the attractions themselves.

2 Prepare an itinerary for a one-day tour in your area for the following:

   (a) a group of senior citizens
   (b) a group of overseas students
   (c) the directors of a company that is considering re-locating its head office to your area.

3 Arrange a visit to a popular tourist attraction in your area and produce a report on the contribution the attraction makes to the local economy. In order to successfully compete this assignment, you will need to interview the attraction manager or their nominee and gather data on the number of visitors and how they spend their money.

CHAPTER 7

THE COUNTRYSIDE

OBJECTIVES

On completion of this chapter, students will be able to:

▶ identify the statutory agencies involved in countryside management and protection

▶ recognise the extent of involvement of the voluntary sector in all aspects of countryside conservation

▶ explain why the involvement of the private sector has been restricted

▶ outline areas where the private sector is becoming increasingly involved and give reasons for such involvement.

Countryside pursuits may be either active or passive and include rambling, hiking, orienteering, mountaineering and rock climbing, although most countryside activities are passive and form a major part of recreational leisure. Indeed, walking is the most popular form of physical recreation.

National government, local authorities and the voluntary sector are all involved in the provision of countryside recreation. The private sector is becoming increasingly active in providing recreational facilities for activities such as private fishing, farm tourism, wildlife parks, private woodland and water sports.

One of the major problems those concerned with countryside recreation face lies in maintaining a happy balance between providing public access to the countryside and conserving the countryside environment: private car ownership has opened up the countryside to town and city dwellers but, as the number of visitors rises, it becomes increasingly difficult to protect the countryside they have come to visit from the environmental damage caused by pollution, erosion and general carelessness and stupidity.

The role of national government

■ THE COUNTRYSIDE COMMISSION

The Countryside Commission was established by the government in 1968 with the passing of The Countryside Act.

The Countryside Commission, like the Sports Council, is a grant in aid body, that is it receives a grant from the government to implement its objective, which is:

'To review matters relating to the conservation and enhancement of landscape beauty in England and Wales, and to the provision and improvement of facilities of the countryside for enjoyment including the need to secure access for open-air recreation.'

The areas of responsibility include:

- the designation of national parks, areas of outstanding natural beauty and long-distance footpaths and bridleways
- to provide grants for country parks, picnic sites and other countryside facilities and services, including planting trees and creating footpaths.
- to undertake research into all areas of countryside management and produce educational and informative literature.

The Countryside Commission provides finance and technical assistance to providing bodies, that is local authorities and national voluntary organisations. Like other government agencies, the amount of grant-in funding is constantly reviewed and it is actively encouraged to put its management services out to private contract.

Figure 7.1
National Parks of England and Wales

The National Parks

There are ten areas in England and Wales designated as National Parks by the Countryside Commission (see Figure 7.1). They cover an area of 5238 square miles (almost a tenth of England and Wales). With the exception of the Lake District and Peak District, which have their own joint planning boards, the National Parks are administered by county council committees. There are two main objectives in this:

- to preserve and enhance the natural beauty and amenities of the Parks
- to promote them to the public.

The National Parks are subject to very rigid planning regulations. Introduction of new industry into the areas may not be allowed on the grounds that it would destroy or damage the countryside and have a detrimental effect on tourism in the area. New buildings must be constructed using local stone and be in keeping with the environment. Facilities such as camping and caravan sites must be shielded from view by trees or hedges – new roads, too, are usually hidden within cuttings. This affects smaller details as well. Any signs erected on buildings, for example, must be approved by the planning committees; there are very strict regulations regarding their size and the materials that can be used to make them.

Tourism within the Parks is managed by creating *honeypots*. These are areas that are deliberately planned to attract tourists, so facilities such as picnic sites, viewpoints, information centres and car parks are concentrated in one area in order to keep the less accessible area unspoilt for the enjoyment of the few who are willing to venture some distance from their cars.

Areas of Outstanding Natural Beauty and Heritage Coasts

In addition to the National Parks, the Countryside Commission designates Areas of Outstanding Natural Beauty and Heritage Coasts. There are currently 37 such areas in England and Wales. There are no statutory arrangements relating to these areas, but local authorities are encouraged to protect them by controlling development and introducing strict planning legislation.

■ THE FORESTRY COMMISSION

The Foresty Commission was established by the Forestry Act in 1919 and is a statutory agency that receives grant in aid from the Department of Agriculture. It is one of the largest landowners in Britain (3 million acres) and is primarily concerned with the production of timber. It maintains seven Forest Parks in Britain and, since 1970, it has employed recreation planning officers to devise and implement recreation plans in each of its regional offices.

The Commission provides viewpoints, picnic sites, car parks, holiday chalets, camping sites and a wide range of recreational activities that are undertaken on its land, including car rallying, horse riding, deer stalking, fishing, hiking, rock climbing, skiing, water sports and nature study.

The Forest Parks and Commission-owned woodlands attract vast numbers of visitors and it is a difficult task to ensure that the recreational pursuits of the public do not interfere with the main tree-felling, planting and conservation activities of the Commission.

■ THE NATURE CONSERVANCY COUNCIL

The Nature Conservancy Council has a similar role to the Forestry Commission in that it controls and manages large areas of national nature reserves. It is an agency of the Department of the Environment.

One of the major roles of the Council is to promote public awareness and understanding of the countryside and nature in order to further their enjoyment of it.

Local authority provision

Local authorities in rural areas have a dual responsibility: on the one hand they need to provide countryside recreation for both their own Council Tax payers and to visitors, but, on the other, they must ensure that the local residents, farmers and other landowners are not inconvenienced by major influxes of day visitors.

Many local authorities are deeply involved in the provision of countryside recreation by having responsibilities for National Parks and/or Areas of Outstanding Natural Beauty and it is a brave director of recreation and leisure services in any county council who does not place emphasis on countryside recreation.

There are over 200 country parks open in Britain. These are maintained by local authorities and provide opportunities for people to enjoy the countryside by providing them with such facilities as car parks, toilets, refreshments and information boards.

The voluntary sector

The voluntary sector is arguably more involved in the provision of recreational facilities and the promotion of recreational activities in the countryside than anywhere else. It is also deeply involved and politically active in the protection of the rural environment.

The following organisations are a selection of some of the more active voluntary organisations, most of which have been granted charitable status:

- The National Trust
- The Council for the Protection of Rural England
- The Royal Society for Nature Conservation
- The Open Spaces Society
- The Ramblers Association
- The Royal Society for the Protection of Birds.

■ THE NATIONAL TRUST

The National Trust was founded in 1885 and looks after properties in England, Wales and Northern Ireland – there is a separate National Trust for Scotland.

In 1907, the Trust was incorporated by an Act of Parliament and set out its aims in the following terms:

'The National Trust shall be established for the purposes of promoting the permanent preservation for the benefit of the nation of lands and tenements (including buildings) of beauty or historic interest and as regards lands for the preservation (so far as practicable) of their natural aspect features and animal and plant life.'

It is a public company but does not trade for profit. It receives no government grant and derives its income from subscriptions, admission charges, gifts and legacies and from trading activities, as well as from rents paid by tenants living in its properties and farming its lands.

After the State and the Crown, the National Trust is the largest landowner in Britain. It owns and manages over 500 000 acres of land in the UK and opens nearly 200 homes and gardens to the public, attracting more than 10 million visitors per year. It owns land that covers the whole spectrum of the word 'countryside', from coastal stretches to woodlands, from downland to hillside areas, and much of the land is agricultural, rented to farmers.

The Trust maintains a Head Office in London and 16 regional offices. It is governed by a National Council consisting of 24 elected members and 24 co-opted members (nominated by institutions with related interests). National Trust policy is decided in council, with advice from regional and central committees. The central committees and panels of the National Trust are:

- Executive Committee
- Properties Committee
- Finance Committee
- Archaeology
- Architecture
- Arts
- Estates
- Gardens
- Nature Conservation
- Enterprises
- Investment Review.

The National Trust is not a political organisation, but, because of the type and number of the properties it owns, it contributes to the general debate on environmental issues and co-operates with the national agencies and other voluntary organisations, particularly over matters concerning conservation and public access to land.

■ THE COUNCIL FOR THE PROTECTION OF RURAL ENGLAND

The Council for the Protection of Rural England was established in 1926 with the following objectives:

- to promote and encourage the improvement, protection and preservation of the English countryside, its towns and villages
- to further appropriate development of the rural environment
- to stimulate and educate public opinion
- to act as a centre for advice and information.

The Council for the Protection of Rural Wales was founded two years later (1928) and has similar objectives.

■ THE ROYAL SOCIETY FOR NATURE CONSERVATION

The Society is concerned with safeguarding wildlife and natural habitats by acquiring and managing sites of national, regional and local significance. It is a sister organisation of the Wildlife Trust.

■ THE OPEN SPACES SOCIETY

The Society (formerly the Commons, Open Spaces and Footpaths Preservation Society) aims to preserve common land for the benefit of the public and assists local authorities to acquire, protect and regulate commons, village greens and open spaces.

■ THE RAMBLERS ASSOCIATION

The Association organises guided walks throughout England and Wales. It acts as a pressure group, campaigning for the rights of walkers in the countryside. Its work particularly concerns the continuation of access to public rights of way across private land. It has a membership in excess of 70 000 and has over 300 local groups.

■ THE ROYAL SOCIETY FOR THE PROTECTION OF BIRDS

This is one of the most well-supported animal charities in the UK. It is concerned with the preservation and protection of wild birds and their habitats. In addition to major campaigns to increase public awareness, it owns and maintains bird sanctuaries.

The private sector

Countryside recreation is possibly the one area of the leisure industry that has not been influenced to a major extent by the private sector. The reasons for this are unclear. It could be argued that it is because much of the land is owned by people or organisations who are more interested in agriculture than leisure. However, it is more likely to be an economic consideration, namely that the private sector is more prepared to invest in urban recreation where there is a large market and a high take-up rate.

Areas in which the private sector are involved are generally concerned with the more profitable or exclusive activities, such as trout and salmon fishing and grouse shooting. In recent years, however, there have been major developments in what is termed *farm tourism*.

Farm tourism is a term that is used to describe the activities farmers have undertaken in order to attract people to the countryside. It includes the conversion of barns and estate cottages to self-catering accommodation, the provision of facilities for caravanning and camping, opening farms to the public (staging demonstrations of farming activities), 'pick your own' farming and the opening of small animal parks (butterfly farms, bird sanctuaries and so on).

Conclusion

Since the creation of urban lifestyles during the Industrial Revolution there has been a yearning on the part of townspeople to take part in recreational activities which are traditionally associated with the countryside and rural life. This has led to the creation of municipal parks and 'green' spaces in cities, by local authorities. Most of the major metropolitan cities in this country have legislation to protect encroaches on the countryside by developers.

National government recognises the importance of the countryside and has created National Parks and 'Areas of Outstanding Natural Beauty' which are protected from tasteless or unnecessary development. Through agencies such as the Countryside Commission and the Forestry Commission there are mechanisms to protect the countryside. Other organisations in both the public and voluntary sectors have been established in order to protect the countryside as a part of our national heritage.

The voluntary sector makes a significant contribution to the leisure-based aspects of the countryside and, through agencies such as the National Trust, serves as both a leisure provider and countryside protector. Many of the voluntary organisations were founded during the latter part of the 19th century as backlash to industrialisation, encouraging people in the towns to retain the rural values of their forebears.

The private sector has become increasingly involved in promoting countryside leisure through the creation of theme-parks and through the expansion of farm tourism. There has also been an increase in the range of privately-run leisure facilities which are based on countryside pursuits. The private sector actively promotes the notion of 'Countryside = healthy lifestyle' in its marketing campaigns.

Assignments

1 Produce a profile of organisations in your area which are concerned with the protection of the countryside. What are their present objectives? When and why were they founded? Have their policies changed in recent years?

2 In most towns and cities there are open spaces which are under threat of re-development and in the countryside, there are frequently planning applications for development of areas of land traditionally open to the public. As a class exercise devise a publicity campaign to protect an area scheduled for re-development. The activities which you could undertake in this exercise are numerous and could include writing letters to the local papers; staging a debate on the proposals; producing a report for submission to the planning committee; setting up a pressure group.

3 Produce a map and promotional leaflet for a walk in an area of the countryside with which you are familiar. Your leaflet should include information on access, the history of the area, and a description of the flora and fauna which are likely to be seen.

CHAPTER 8

MARKETING IN THE LEISURE INDUSTRY

OBJECTIVES

On completion of this chapter, students will be able to:

▶ understand the contribution which marketing makes to the success of a leisure organisation

▶ recognise the different techniques applied to marketing goods and services

▶ identify the key elements of the marketing process

▶ device a marketing plan for promoting a leisure event or service.

What is marketing?

'Marketing is the management process responsible for identifying, anticipating and satisfying customer requirements profitably.'

The Institute of Marketing

In business terms, marketing provides an integrated approach to the planning, pricing, promotion, distribution and servicing of products and services in order to establish and maintain profitability – in other words, marketing is the business of *creating* a market.

Marketing of leisure is undertaken by all those who provide services, resources and goods for the industry, whether they are working in the private, public or voluntary sectors. There are differences in approach and attitude to marketing that are dependent on the philosophies or objectives of the organisations concerned. There are also differences in the marketing techniques that are applied. These vary according to the type of product being marketed and, of course, the amount of money available.

Marketing in the private sector is a sophisticated, imaginative, multimillion-pound industry and its influence may be seen everywhere. It would be unfair to suggest that the public and voluntary sectors are unsophisticated and unimaginative or that they fail to influence the public to use their facilities, but more that until relatively recently the need for marketing in the public and voluntary sectors was thought unnecessary. The growth of leisure (creating greater competition) has made it increasingly important – particularly for local authorities – to ensure that their facilities are fully used and do not become a drain on the limited funds available for leisure provision.

Leisure services would not exist without customers. In the past, many companies and organisations were *product orientated,* producing goods and services that *they* thought the public wanted and, in the absence of competition, people would continue to buy the products regardless of their quality. This used to be the case with local authority swimming pools, with few exceptions: with a specific geographical sector of the community in mind (it was considered, quite rightly, that swimming was beneficial to everyone), many of the larger local authorities provided pools without first carrying out any market research and only a little consultation. They were all very similar and consumers seldom considered using a pool in a neighbouring town. In recent years, however, leisure pools, offering a variety of recreational facilities, have been developed by both the private and public sectors. Customers have shown their preferences by using the better facilities in neighbouring areas, forcing the owners of other facilities to look at the services they provide and increase their levels and standards of marketing.

What does marketing involve?

Marketing identifies customer needs and wants and provides them at the right price. It is not limited to products in development or new ones but is also used to ensure that the sales of existing products are maintained or improved.

There are differences in the ways *services* are marketed compared to *goods,* largely because goods are *manufactured,* whereas services are *performed.*

Services are intangible. They cannot be inspected before use, they can only be experienced. For example, a travel agent cannot sell a holiday 'on approval' for 10 days, nor can the customer return it if it is not suitable. Similarly, the FA Cup Final cannot be staged at any time and the spectator cannot demand money back if the teams do not play to their usual standards. Users of a leisure centre expect high standards of service from staff and they will expect the facilities to be clean and tidy. If they are not, they are unlikely to return when there are alternative, better-resourced facilities in the area, but they have to experience the facilities before they can know this or have received reports from others who have experienced them.

Services cannot be stored and have a limited lifespan. For example, cinema managers hire films in advance and screen them at specified times of the day during the period of hire. If there is a heatwave, people will want to be outdoors, but the screenings cannot be held over until it rains, the films must be paid for. Also, leisure centres are usually open all the year round but are used most in the evenings, at weekends and during the school holidays. From an economics viewpoint, closing centres during the daytime, on weekdays or during term time might seem logical, but those customers who use the centre outside peak times would be lost.

Services are performed on the producers' premises with customer participation. The customer travels to the place of performance.

Services are inconsistent. Manufacturers of goods can introduce quality control systems to ensure a consistent standard, but the service industry relies on staff to provide a consistent service.

Ownership of services is temporary. Purchase of a service involves the right to use a service at a fixed time and place. A game of squash involves the hire and use of a court for a limited period of time. The consumer pays for the *use* of the court rather than for the *court* itself. Once the time hired has elapsed, the game ceases and players must leave the court, regardless of whether or not it is finished.

The key elements of marketing

These are:

- assessing the market
- pricing strategies
- product placement
- product promotion.

■ ASSESSING THE MARKET

The process of assessing the market is known as *market research*. In order to operate successfully, a leisure organisation needs to be fully aware of the market and be able to answer the following questions:

- What are the customers' needs and wants?
- What is the size of the market?
- What is the competition?
- How much are the public prepared to pay for the facilities on offer?
- What is the value of the market, will it be profitable?
- How much will it cost to meet customer needs and wants?

The aim of market research is to find out the answers to these questions. Larger organisations will have their own market research departments, but, for the smaller organisation, it is necessary to either employ a market research consultant or to carry out their own research. The research undertaken takes two forms: *desk research* and *practical research*.

Desk research involves researching information that has already been gathered and published by other organisations or individuals. Practical research requires information that does not exist to be gathered by finding out the needs, wants and opinions of clients through observation, questionnaire research and interviews.

■ PRICING STRATEGIES

The following are some of the most commonly applied pricing strategies.

For market penetration

- *Low prices* encourage people to use a facility – this is particularly relevant when establishing a market for a new product, service or facility.
- *Loss leader pricing* – selling products or services at a loss – is used to attract customers on to the site, then, once the customers are on site, they are encouraged to use other, more profitable facilities.
- *Discount pricing* involves offering goods or services at a reduced rate, either for certain types of groups of customers or at certain times.
- *Variable pricing* is varying the prices charged for different customers, which may mean, for example, offering lower (discounted) prices to senior citizens or other unwaged customers.

Pricing for profit

- *Short-term profit maximisation* involves setting the price at as high a level as the market is prepared to pay in order to make as much profit as possible as quickly as possible. It is only possible to maintain this in the short term as, once other competitors move into the market-place, the price will fall.

This strategy is often used when a unique but potentially very popular product or service is introduced. It takes into account the importance of trends or fashion in leisure. An organisation that is the first to introduce squash, ten pin bowling or a fitness suite in an area may, in the first instance, charge high prices as there is no competition. However, as other leisure organisations introduce similar, possibly improved, facilities, the price will fall.

- *High price maintenance* takes advantage of the 'snob value' of products or services. Some customers see high prices as a reflection of quality and status and are prepared to pay, for example, high membership fees to a sports club based on its location, the social standing of its members and the exclusivity of membership.

It may also be seen as a strategy to ensure genuine quality of services to a select few rather than lower priced mediocre service to a mass market.

■ **PRODUCT PLACEMENT**

Product placement involves the distribution of goods and services – how they are made available to customers – and includes:

- Channels of distribution
- Accessibility
- Location.

It is important to remember that leisure is a service industry and that, generally, customers travel to the facilities rather than having them brought to their home or workplace.

Channels of distribution

Most products are sold through third parties (wholesaler, retailers or agents), but services are generally sold or provided directly to the public, with the advantage that the owner of the facility has control over how the service is presented to the public. The quality of service can be readily gauged by obtaining direct feedback from customers.

Accessibility

Leisure services are generally made available to as many people as possible, although there are some organisations that prefer to remain exclusive.

Location
Regardless of how well a leisure facility is presented to the public in terms of price, quality of service or successful promotion, the facility will only be successful if it is easily accessible. If the facility is not well signposted, lacks sufficient parking spaces or is not easy to get to by car or public transport, it is more likely to fail than succeed as it will be unable to attract sufficient numbers and will be less able to compete against better-resourced facilities in the area.

■ PRODUCT PROMOTION

Product promotion is the most widely recognised aspect of marketing. It is the part of the marketing mix that is concerned with communicating with existing and potential customers about the products and services an organisation provides.

Promotion aims to:

- create customer awareness and understanding
- encourage participation
- create customer preference
- encourage repeat business.

In the process of promotion, customers are attracted to a facility by means of advertising, publicity and public relations, using words, music, pictures and symbols to present a positive image of the product, service or facility.

Advertising
Advertising can be expensive. A short television commercial shown at peak times across the nation will cost thousands of pounds to screen. Additionally, costs are involved in producing the advertisement.

A full-page advertisement in a national newspaper will cost in the region of £30 000 and even in a local newspaper such an advertisement can cost several thousand pounds – far more than most smaller leisure organisations are able to afford. National advertising is restricted, generally, to larger, private-sector organisations that manufacture goods rather than provide services.

Local advertising is important as it reaches the people most likely to make use of the facilities on offer. It is not restricted to newspaper and radio campaigns, but includes other activities such as mail shots, handouts, give-away sales gimmicks, special offers, incentives and sponsorship. Indeed, it includes almost any activity that is likely to publicise the organisation in a positive way without breaking the law, so the scope is wide.

Public relations   Public relations is the cheapest form of advertising.

The media (newspapers, radio and television) are major influencers of public taste and those who work in the leisure industry must always be aware of the 'power of the press'. It is essential to maintain a good working relationship with local radio, television and newspaper journalists and be able to influence the image-making process by turning opportunity to advantage: a good news story produces free advertising and good publicity.

Marketing check-list

1 Know your company – its activities, staff and organisational structure.

2 Know your business – its strengths and weaknesses, its commercial aims and objectives.

3 *Know your customers* – who they are, where they live, what they like to do, when they like to do it.

4 Know your competitors – their facilities, activities and programmes, Identify *their* strengths and weaknesses as their weaknesses may provide you with opportunities.

5 Keep up to date with events in the leisure industry.

6 Make use of public relations. Make friends with the press and decision makers in the community.

7 Plan your marketing meticulously and review its effects regularly.

8 Create and maintain a positive public image of your organisation. Make sure, for example, that your staff are trained in how to communicate with and show care and consideration for your customers.

9 Support local charities and organisations.

10 Put the customer first.

11 Keep your facilities clean, well-maintained, attractive, colourful, well signposted and safe.

12 Make the facilities accessible to your market.

13 Keep the public informed of your activities.

14 Make sure that any publicity is legal, honest, decent and truthful.

15 Be objective.

Advertising check-list

Who is your target audience?

What are you advertising?

When will you advertise?

Where will you place the advertisements?

Why are you advertising?

How will you evaluate your results?

How much will it cost?

What alternative strategies have you considered?

Conclusion

Marketing is a business discipline, the purpose of which is to ensure that a market is created and maintained. The leisure industry, being orientated towards the provision of *services* rather than the production of *goods,* needs to focus its marketing activities on the standard, quality and range of services it offers, placing considerable emphasis on customer care.

Marketeers in leisure need to know not only the size of their markets, but be aware of the changing needs and wants of the local community. This is achieved by means of desk research, (statistical analysis and demographic studies) and obtaining direct feedback from customers.

As a result of market research, leisure providers are able to make decisions on the pricing strategies and promotional activities that are aimed at attracting and maintaining appropriate levels of participation by their clients.

Marketing is frequently a very expensive business activity, although it need not be so. Public relations are as important as advertising, if not more so. The leisure industry, being a customer-orientated industry, must cultivate the local media in order to ensure that the public are aware of the leisure services that are available in an area.

Assignments

1   Compare and contrast the marketing strategies adopted by a local authority-run leisure facility in your area and a comparable private-sector leisure provider.

2   Referring to the business plan you prepared as an assignment at the end of Chapter 4, Finance, produce a marketing plan for the company. This should include examples of display advertising, publicity handouts and a policy for dealing with representatives of the media.

3   Prepare and implement a marketing campaign for the BTEC National or GNVQ Leisure Studies course you are taking. In order to complete this assignment, you will need to make use of the Marketing and Advertising check-lists in this chapter. To support your campaign, produce or obtain suitable course information, mount a display for use either on a college open day or for taking to secondary schools in the area and prepare a verbal presentation.

CHAPTER 9

ART AND ENTERTAINMENT

OBJECTIVES

On completion of this chapter the students will be able to:

▶ Identify the wide range of activities which come under the umbrella of Art and Entertainment

▶ Outline the contribution made to the industry by national Government through the activities of the Arts Council

▶ Explain the duties of a local authority in the provision of Art and Entertainment

▶ Recognise and account for the extent of involvement of the private sector in the entertainment industry.

Included under the umbrella of art and entertainment are many popular leisure activities. Tourism, countryside activities, sport and physical recreation, essentially, take place outdoors whereas the majority of art and entertainment activities take place indoors, many of them in the home. The home-based ones are provided, predominantly, by the private sector, such as programmes on radio and television, video and hi-fi equipment, hobby accessories, art and craft materials, books, newspapers, magazines and so on. Art and entertainment in the community is often provided by local authorities, voluntary organisations and the commercial sector and includes the following:

- art galleries
- exhibitions
- bingo
- dancing
- theatre
- cinema
- concerts
- museums
- nightclubs
- social events

The role of the government

The Government is an art and entertainment enabler rather than a provider.

The Ministry for the Arts is a division of the Department of National Heritage. Principal art galleries and museums such as the British Museum and the National Portrait Gallery are funded by the government and are run by civil servants. Admission to national museums and galleries is free of charge, although most are now requesting voluntary donations on entry.

Figure 9.1
British Museum
(Courtesy of the
British Museum)

■ THE ARTS COUNCIL

The Arts Council of Great Britain was established in 1946 by Royal Charter and is a receiver of grant in aid from the Government. It has three main objectives:

- to develop and improve the knowledge, understanding and practice of the arts
- to increase the accessibility of the arts to the public throughout Great Britain
- to co-operate with governments, local authorities and other bodies to achieve these objectives.

Its activities are widespread and include:

- providing financial aid to appropriately constituted arts organisations
- co-operation with district councils, local education authorities and other educational institutions in fulfilling the obligation for cultural action placed on them by legislation
- organising tours (drama, opera, ballet and so on) throughout the country in association with local authorities, arts committees and promoting societies
- encouraging district councils and educational agencies in the improvement of existing facilities and the provision of new facilities for the performance and practice of the arts.

The Arts Council assists the promotion of the visual arts, drama, film, video and broadcasting, music, literature and dance.

In recent years, almost a third of the Arts Council's money has been spent on subsidising the national arts companies, which are:

- The Royal Opera House
- The English National Opera
- The Royal Ballet
- The National Theatre
- The Royal Shakespeare Company.

In 1984, the Government introduced the Business Sponsorship Incentive Scheme (BSIS), which matched grants for new sponsorship. As a result, Arts Council projects have received sponsorship from over 900 companies.

Local authority provision

Local authorities provide art and entertainment on the strength of three Acts of Parliament:

- the Public Libraries and Museums Act 1964 made it a *duty* to provide library services and gives *permission* for the provision of museum services
- the Education Act 1944 made it a *duty* for local authorities to provide for adult education and youth services
- the Local Government Act 1972 gives *permission* for the provision of entertainment and cultural activities and events.

As a result of this, the extent of provision of art and entertainment varies considerably from one local authority to another.

Local authorities have a key role in the co-ordination of arts and entertainment activities in their area. This is because they provide a whole range of activities via adult education, youth services, letting of facilities to local groups, managing theatres, arts centres, museum and library services (through which they are able to make a contribution towards home-based art and entertainment). It is important to remember that the local authority's responsibility in art and entertainment is towards the community and it must, therefore, provide facilities for all ages.

Children receive their first introductions to different kinds of arts and entertainment at home, then through their schools' programmes. Outside the school environment, art and entertainment is provided by a youth service that organises community activities for secondary school-aged children. For those who have left school, the arts are generally provided either through adult education or through museums and libraries.

For senior citizens and the socially disadvantaged, access to the arts is an area that receives priority in local authorities' plans. It is provided by the relevant departments, but may receive additional assistance from the Social Services Department.

■ LICENSING

One of the key ways in which the local authority is involved with art and entertainment is licensing. In order to provide public social entertainment events, there are various licences that may be required and numerous regulations have to be observed.

The regulations that particularly affect art and entertainment activities relate to public entertainment, theatres and cinemas.

Public entertainment licence (PEL)

A PEL is required in most parts of the country where public dancing, live music or similar kinds of entertainment take place, excepting fairgrounds and circuses, places of public religious worship, garden fêtes and bazaars. There are also regulations regarding the licensing of entertainments that take place wholly or mainly in the open air on private land.

Theatre licences

No premises may be used for a public performance without a licence. The Theatres Act 1968 defines a play as being any dramatic event given wholly or in part by live performers. It includes ballet and open-air theatre.

Performances that require licences must be open to the general public regardless of whether or not there is an admission charge.

Cinema licence

A licence is required for any regular cinema performance open to the general public.

Regulations

In addition to the above there are many other regulations (particularly regarding public health and safety and access) that need to be observed.

What the private sector provides

■ HOME-BASED ACTIVITIES

In order to see the extent of what the private sector provides by way of home-based activities, it is useful to look at some of the statistics published by the Government (see, too Figure 8.1):

Figure 9.2
Private-sector participation in home-based activities (General Household Survey 1989–90)

- 99% of households own a television set
- 60% of households own a video recorder
- in 1989, 8 million video tapes were hired out per week
- most people watch television for almost 25 hours per week
- in 1989, CD sales exceeded those of LPs for the first time.

The private sector is able to capitalise on public events by promoting video, CD, record and tape sales, selling television rights and merchandising associated goods, effectively bringing outside entertainment into the home (few rock concerts would show a profit without the extra income they generate in this manner).

■ PUBLIC ENTERTAINMENT

Private-sector entertainment activities can be divided into two main areas: those that require active participation (ballrooms, nightclubs, bingo halls and so on) and those that are performed *to* audiences and spectators (cinemas, theatres, concerts, live shows and cabaret).

■ CINEMA

The General Household Survey of 1987 stated that the cinema was the most popular of the audience-type activities, with 11 per cent of the population going to the cinema compared to 7 per cent to the theatre and only 1 per cent to the opera or ballet. It would appear that attendance at art and entertainment venues is very much class-based, with a lower proportion of people from the unskilled, manual occupations attending than those from professional occupations. It would also seem that professional people are far more likely to visit art galleries or museums.

The production, distribution, showing of films and cinema ownership is in the hands of a few companies (notably Thorn EMI and Rank) and there are now very few independent cinemas. In the 1990s, ownership of the major film corporations changed, with substantial investment in the film market coming from major Japanese corporations like Sony.

■ THEATRE

There are approximately 120 professional theatres in the UK. Half of these are owned by the private sector, the majority of them being in the West End of London. The West End theatres attract around 11 million vistors a year, but because the tickets are expensive, the majority of West End theatre goers are from overseas.

Generally speaking, the theatre is not a profitable market for the private sector. There are two main reasons for this. First, the high fees commanded by star performers (who can make even more money working in television or film) and, second, the high levels of subsidy received by the national companies make it extremely difficult for the commercial sector to compete. For these reasons, many of the more popular shows in the West End are musicals. Although they are extremely expensive to stage, they can be supported by the additional sales of records, tapes, CDs and other merchandise. These musicals require a large stage set and have large casts so that it makes them difficult to stage in the smaller provincial theatres.

Assignment 1

From the following extracts taken from Social Trends 22 (HMSO, 1992), produce a report on home-based leisure activities.

Availability of leisure time

Time use in a typical week: by employment status and sex, 1990–91

Great Britain   Hours

	Full-time employees		Part-time employees		
	Males	Females	Females	Housewives	Retired
Weekly hours spent on:					
Employment and travel[1]	48.3	42.6	20.9	0.3	0.7
Essential activities[2]	24.1	39.6	52.1	58.4	33.0
Sleep[3]	49.0	49.0	49.0	49.0	49.0
Free time	46.6	36.8	46.0	60.3	85.3
Free time per weekday	4.5	3.3	5.4	8.4	11.6
Free time per weekend day	12.1	10.3	9.5	9.3	13.6

1 Travel to and from place of work
2 Essential domestic work and personal care, including essential
   shopping, child care, cooking, personal hygiene and appearance.
3 An average of 7 hours sleep per night is assumed

Source: The Henley Centre for Forecasting

Weekly hours of work and entitlement to annual paid holidays[1]

United Kingdom

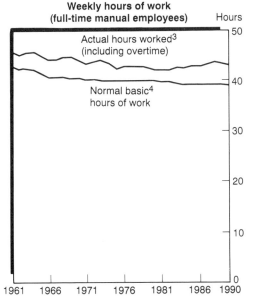

**Weekly hours of work
(full-time manual employees)**

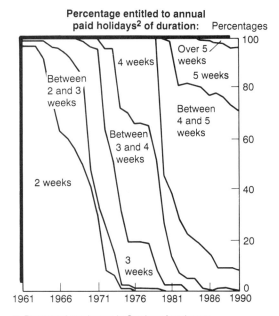

**Percentage entitled to annual
paid holidays[2] of duration:**

1 Under the Wages Act, 1986 (and similar legislation in
   Northern Ireland) Wages Councils are no longer empowered
   to fix holidays. From 1987, employees covered by Wages
   Councils are excluded from the holiday figures which are
   not therefore directly compatible with earlier ones.
2 The information relates to basic entitlements in national
   collective agreements or Wages Council Orders.

3 By manual employees in October of each year.
4 The information relates to basic hours in national
   collective agreements or Wages Council Orders.

Source: Employment Department

Home-based leisure activities

Leisure based consumer durables: by household type, 1989–90

Great Britain   Percentages

	1 adult aged 16–59	2 adults aged 16–59	Small family[1]	Large family[2]	Large adult house-hold[3]	2 adults 1 or both aged 60 and over	1 adult aged 60 and over	All house-holds
Percentage of households with								
Television	94	99	99	99	100	99	98	99
Video cassette recorder	48	78	81	82	84	39	11	60
Home computer	10	15	37	46	31	4	1	19
Compact disc player	15	21	17	21	28	7	2	15

1   One or 2 persons aged 16 and over and 1 or 2 persons aged under 16.
2   One or more persons aged 16 and over and 3 or more persons aged under 16,
    or 3 or more persons aged 16 and over and 2 persons aged under 16.
3   Three or more persons aged 16 and over, with or without 1 person aged under 16.

Source: General Household Survey

Television viewing[1]: by social class

United Kingdom   Hours and minutes and percentages

	1986	1987	1988	1989	1990
Social class[2]					
(hours: minutes per week)					
ABC1	20:47	20:54	20:14	19:48	19:31
C2	25:18	24:40	25:25	25:00	24:13
DE	33:11	31:47	31:44	30:57	30:13
All persons	25:54	25:25	25:21	24:44	23:51
Reach[3]					
(percentages)					
Daily	78	76	77	78	77
Weekly	94	93	94	94	94

1   Viewing of live television broadcasts from the BBC, ITV and Channel 4.   2 See Appendix, Part 10: Social class.
3   Percentage of UK population aged 4 and over who viewed TV for at least three consecutive minutes.

Source: Broadcasters' Audience Research Board; British Broadcasting Corporation; AGB Limited

Radio listening: by age

Hours and minutes and percentages
United Kingdom

	1986	1987	1988	1989	1990
Age group					
(hours: minutes per week)					
4–15 years	2:12	2:07	2:13	2:21	2:26
16–34	11:24	11:18	11:40	12:07	12:28
35–64	9:56	10:16	10:33	11:10	11:42
65 years and over	8:27	8:44	8:49	9:00	9:18
All aged 4 years and over	8:40	8:52	9:12	9:46	10:12
Reach[1] *(percentages)*					
Daily	43	43	43	44	45
Weekly	75	74	73	74	74

1   Percentage of UK population aged 4 and over who listened to radio for at
    least half a programme a day
Source: British Broadcasting Corporation

Television viewing: by type of programme, 1990

United Kingdom

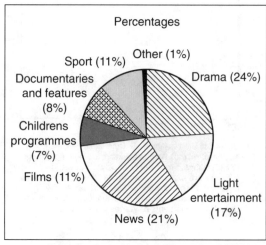

Percentages

Sport (11%) Other (1%)
Documentaries and features (8%)
Childrens programmes (7%)
Films (11%)
Drama (24%)
Light entertainment (17%)
News (21%)

Source: Broadcasters' Audience Research Board; AGB Limited

Hiring of pre-recorded VCR tapes

United Kingdom

	1986	1988	1989	1990
Domestic video population[1] (millions)	9.66	12.20	13.80	14.80
Hiring of video tapes[2] *Percentage hiring tapes during previous 7 days*	30	29	30	26
Average number of tapes per hiring	2.24	2.02	1.94	1.90
Number of tapes hired per week (millions)	6.5	7.2	8.0	7.3

1 Estimated number of households in possession of at least one video cassette recorder based on a survey of 13,000 households per quarter.
2 Figures refer to households in possession of a video cassette recorder.

Source: British Videogram Association

Trade deliveries of LPs, cassettes, compact discs and singles[1]

United Kingdom

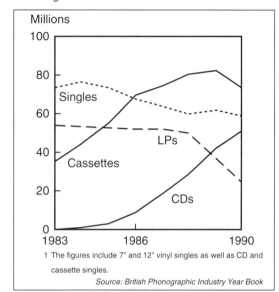

1 The figures include 7" and 12" vinyl singles as well as CD and cassette singles.

Source: British Phonographic Industry Year Book

Reading of the most popular magazines: by sex and age, 1971 and 1990

Great Britain

	Percentage of adults reading each magazine in 1990			Percentage of each age group reading each magazine in 1990				Readership[1] (millions)		Readers per copy (numbers)
	Males	Females	All adults	15–24	25–44	45–64	65 and over	1971	1990	1990
General magazines										
Radio Times	18	19	19	20	20	18	17	9.5	8.5	2.9
TV Times	18	19	19	21	19	18	15	9.9	8.4	3.0
Reader's Digest	14	13	13	8	13	17	14	9.2	6.1	3.9
What Car	7	1	4	6	5	3	1		1.8	12.2
National Geographic	5	3	4	4	4	4	2	1.1	1.7	
Exchange and Mart	5	2	3	5	4	3	1		1.5	8.2
Women's magazines[2]										
Woman's Own	3	16	10	10	11	9	8	7.2	4.3	4.2
Bella	3	15	10	12	11	8	6		4.3	
Women's Weekly	2	11	7	4	5	9	10	4.7	3.1	2.6
Woman	2	11	7	6	8	6	5	8.0	3.0	3.2
Best	2	11	6	9	8	5	3		2.9	3.1
Prima	2	10	6	7	8	5	2		2.6	3.0

1 Defined as the average issue readership and represents the number of people who claim to have read, or looked at, one or more copies of a given publication during a period equal to the interval at which the publication appears.

2 The age analysis for women's magazines includes male readers.

Source: National Readership Surveys, Joint Industry Committee for National Readership Surveys; Circulation Review, Audit Bureau of Circulation

Public entertainment

Attendances at West End theatre performances

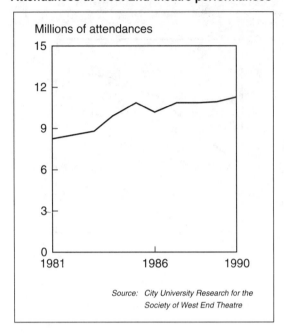

Millions of attendances

Source: City University Research for the
Society of West End Theatre

Attendance at cinemas[1]: by age

United Kingdom					Percentages
	1984	1986	1988	1989	1990
Aged					
7–14	73	87	84	85	85
15–24	59	82	81	86	87
25–34	49	65	64	72	79
35–44	45	60	61	67	70
45 and over	13	25	34	35	41
All persons aged 7 and over	38	53	56	60	64

1 Percentage attending at least once in any given year.

Source: Cinema and Video Audience Research

Assignment 2

It has often been suggested that the Arts Council of Great Britain places too much emphasis on the subsidy of 'high culture' (opera, ballet and symphony orchestras, for example) and that it does not do enough to 'bring the arts to the people'.

■ **TASK**

Using information contained in the Annual Reports of either the Arts Council of Great Britain or your Regional Arts Council make notes for a class discussion on the future role of the Arts Council and the contribution it should make to 'popular culture'.

Assignment 3

The responsibilities of the recently formed Department of National Heritage include the administration of a 'Millenium Fund'.

■ **TASK**

Produce an outline plan for a *Millenium Festival of Art and Entertainment* in your area. This plan should include suggestions for the venue, promotion and sponsorship and should encourage local arts clubs, societies and cultural associations to participate in the event.

In order to maintain their audience levels, cinema owners are now having to invest in the latest projection equipment and luxury multiscreen auditoriums. Multiplex cinemas are being built on the outskirts of large towns and cities where generous car parks can be provided easily.

Conclusion

National Goverment provides financial assistance to the Arts through the intermediary of the Arts Council. The structure of the Arts Council is developed to regional committees and substantial, though inadequate funding of the Arts is maintained through this mechanism. A large proportion of Arts Council funding is given towards the subsidy of National Opera, Ballet and Theatre.

The extent of the provision of art and entertainment facilities by local authorities varies considerably. However, all local authorities have statutory duties to provide particular facilities and are empowered to use their discretion in other areas.

Local authorities have only statutory duties, which have a major effect on local art and entertainment provision, with regard to the licensing of theatres and cinemas and other places of public entertainment.

The private sector is a major provider of entertainment. Since the advent of radio and television its spheres of activity have expanded.

CHAPTER 10

WORKING IN THE LEISURE INDUSTRY

No book can really tell you what it is like to work in the leisure industry and this chapter is not intended to tell you how to get a job. It simply looks at some aspects of employment in the industry – the advantages and disadvantages of the work, career structures and training opportunities – and gives some ideas on how to find out more about it.

Working in the leisure industry is different! Remember, leisure is a *service* industry and is concerned first and foremost with *people,* but there are other factors that make it different.

As leisure activities take so many different forms, the opportunities for employment are wide and varied. If, for example, you are employed as a leisure assistant by a local authority, you could be working in a museum or art gallery as a curator, guide, on a souvenir stall or as a receptionist, but you could, equally, be working as a lifeguard, instructor or attendant in a swimming pool, as a warden in a county park or as a youth leader in the education department. For every job that involves direct contact with the public, there are as many 'backroom' employees dealing with administration, technical support, maintenance and so on who may seldom, if ever, come into contact with the public. These and a wide variety of other jobs present many opportunities for employment in the industry. Indeed, looking at leisure employment in its broadest sense and being aware that statistics can be misleading, approximately 8 per cent of the total workforce in the UK are employed in leisure or its related industries.

Working in leisure has its problems. Ask yourself:

- Am I prepared to work long, unsocial hours?
- Do I enjoy working in the evenings and at weekends when others are enjoying their leisure?
- Am I willing to work shifts?
- Would I consider working a six-day week?

- Do I want a job that includes periods of intense activity followed by long periods of relative calm?
- Am I able to work with others as part of a team?

Shift work

The leisure industry relies on employees who are prepared to work on a shift system rather than 'normal' office hours because:

- facilities are open for periods of time that are too long to be covered by one person
- unsocial hours (those outside the standard 9am to 5pm) are worked when the general public is at leisure, so it would not be practicable for one person to work every single night or every weekend
- safety requirements demand a high level of awareness and working long hours without breaks adversely affects concentration and efficiency.

■ THE ADVANTAGES OF SHIFT WORK

These are:

- some employees enjoy a system where working times are flexible
- employees are working with the general public, have contact with different sets of people and may be required to carry out a number of different activities during the working session
- having days off when others are working can have its advantages, particularly with regard to travel and shopping
- shift work is flexible and creates many opportunities for other activities, such as further education
- there are usually plenty of opportunities to earn overtime!

■ THE DISADVANTAGES OF SHIFT WORK

These are:

- unsocial hours interfere with regular activities (this is particularly a problem if, for example, you have regular commitment to a sports team, club or social activity)
- maintaining contact with friends who work normal office hours may be difficult

- employees might miss out on family life, spending little time, for example, with very young children
- working on early or late shifts may create problems with public transport (many employers appreciate this, however, and will provide transport)
- it can be difficult to sleep during the day!

Seasonality

With some notable exceptions, much of the leisure industry is seasonal. This does not mean that a leisure facility will close down completely during its closed season, but it does mean that many workers are taken on for the peak season only and that a skeleton staff is employed the rest of the time, involved very much behind the scenes with administration and maintenance, planning and publicity.

For many people, the seasonal aspect of a job is particularly appealing. Thousands of students over the years have been able to add to their grant income by working in the leisure industry during the summer vacation. Seasonal work gives you an ideal introduction to the industry and provides that 'previous experience' so often a requirement for full-time or permanent work. There are many examples of directors of recreation and leisure services, large tour operators and famous entertainers who received their introduction to the industry by working a summer season in a leisure centre as a sports assistant, in an overseas resort as a courier or resort representative or in a holiday camp as a 'redcoat'.

Seasonal work is not necessarily well paid, although there may be valuable perks that can make up for this.

Finding out about employment in the leisure industry

If you are already enrolled on a full-time Leisure Studies Course, you will have many opportunities to find out about working in the leisure industry in your talks with course tutors, visiting speakers and through work experience. Your college careers office and library will have further information on education and training opportunities and you will find out more through your assignment work and by visiting leisure facilities near you.

Make the most of any opportunities to find out as much about the industry as possible. This is necessary whether you have already identified a career path to follow and have determined a set of personal goals and objectives or you are still unsure of what you wish to do when you finish your course. Here are some ideas:

- consider finding part-time work, but *only* if you feel you can cope with the demands of your course *and* those of your employer
- look for a holiday job in the industry
- talk to people already employed in the industry
- write to professional organisations for advice and information
- read articles about the industry, produced from within and outside it, so you know about new developments and what job opportunities they present.

Do you have the personal qualities to work in the industry?

Ask yourself:

- Am I a skilled communicator?
- Am I well-organised and efficient?
- Am I able to work on my own initiative?
- Am I interested in people?
- Am I adaptable?
- Do I work well with others?
- Can I motivate other people?
- Can I recognise and cope with emergencies?
- Can I carry out instructions?
- Do I like working with the general public?
- Do I have leadership qualities?
- Do I have a sense of humour?

What other personal qualities do you possess that you think will help you to succeed in leisure? The industry looks for multitalented people to manage multimillion pound high-tech facilities. This requires high-profile managers with financial, technical and interpersonal skills who are willing to work round the clock to ensure that their customers – regardless of age, gender, ethnic origin or abilities – are happy.

Training

Training for employment in the leisure industry is becoming increasingly important, although it is still possible to work your way up to management positions and there are opportunities for gaining professional qualifications while you do so.

■ OPTIONS

Pupils who leave school at 16+ without academic qualifications can take the following courses:

- City and Guilds 481 (Recreation and Leisure Studies)
- BTEC First Diploma/Certificate in Leisure Studies.
- GNVQ Level 2 in Leisure and Tourism

Pupils who leave school having passed some GCSEs can take the following courses:

- BTEC National Diploma/Certificate in Leisure Studies
- BTEC National Diploma/Certificate in Travel and Tourism
- BTEC National Diploma/Certificate in Business Studies.
- GNVQ Level 3 in Leisure and Tourism

Pupils who leave school with a minimum of 1 A-level can take the following courses:

- BTEC Higher National Diploma/Certificate in Leisure Studies or associated disciplines
- CNAA and university degrees in Leisure, Recreation Management, Tourism, Business Studies or associated disciplines.

Graduates can take the following:

- CNAA diplomas
- masters degrees.

'In service' courses include:

- City and Guilds Courses
- BTEC Certificate Courses.

These may be studied for on a part-time basis at an evening class or on a day-release basis.

There are numerous opportunities for gaining appropriate qualifications by means of part-time study and employers may be prepared to contribute to all or part of the costs of study.

Conclusion

Whatever field you decide to pursue, you will find that if you have the right personal qualities and are prepared to work hard to achieve your personal goals, leisure is one of the most dynamic and rewarding industries to work in.

Assignments

1 What do you wish to do when you have finished your course?

2 Produce a career path for the next three stages of your career.

3 What will you have to do to achieve your goals?

4 What skills do you already possess?

5 What skills do you need to develop?

6 What further information do you require?

7 Where will you obtain the information?

8 When and how will you obtain it?

EDNEY DOWN

Edney Down is a small village which lies on the banks of the River Lee. It has a population of 900. It is a village which dates back to Norman times when William the Conqueror granted land, grazing and fishing rights to Baron Peter de Gwynne whose descendent, Lord Gwynne, is Lord of the Manor. His ancestral home, Kinnerley Hall, is situated on the B4026, 1 mile west of the village.

Today Edney Down is a dormitory village. In the 1980s there was a major influx of *yuppies* who bought houses in the area which are used mainly at the weekends when the village leaps into life. The village pubs are particular attractions.

Two miles North-East of the village there is another large estate which until 1960 belonged to the late Sir Walter Elkin. In order to avoid death duties Sir Walter bequeathed the estate to the National Trust who are now considering imposing a ban on fox hunting on the estate, much to the dismay of the hunt and of the local farmers who are tenants of the trust and hunt supporters. There are six farms on the Elkin Estate, four mixed (arable and dairy) and two hill farms (sheep).

The village is dominated by St Marks Church, a magnificent Elizabethan church famous for the tombs of wealthy woollen merchants. The church has a 200-foot tower and is located 300 yards north of Market Square on Peasecod Street; it contains the family vaults of the de Gwynne and de Jacob families.

Penfold, Shearers and Flock Streets are reminders of these happier, more prosperous times. The exceptionally wide High Street which leads into Market Square indicates that the village was once a thriving market town. The Market Cross is in need of restoration.

One mile South-East of the village there is a commemorative stone to the Battle of Edney Down where the Royalists were defeated by the Cromwellian Army during the English Civil War. Recently some village schoolchildren found a purse of silver coins on the common.

This has meant that the land is invaded by treasure hunters with metal detectors at the weekends. Although no more treasure troves have been discovered, several swords, musket balls and belt buckles have been unearthed. The Parish Council, who are responsible for the upkeep of the land, are concerned about the amount of damage which is being caused.

The village school, Chisholms, has 90 pupils. It is a primary school and was founded in 1593 by William Chisholm. Situated on Chisholm Street, 120 yards west of Market Square, the school is under threat of closure. If it closes, pupils will have to be bussed to Milltown 12 miles away. The closure of the school will also mean that many of the village's recreation and leisure facilities would be under threat since the school hall is used for badminton and as an annexe for the Milltown Adult Education Institute. The Chisholm legacy states that the site must be used for educational purposes.

The village is dying on its feet! Yet, there is some hope. The Parish Council have invited local business people to a meeting of local residents where they will be putting forward proposals to develop the village into a small town. This is a long-term project and would be unlikely to happen before the year 2000.

The following factors should be taken into account in considering the project:

1. *Whilst Edney Down is in decline, Milltown is expanding rapidly.* A superstore has been built on the A347 Milltown – Edney Down Road and the village shopkeepers have noticed a significant drop in their volume of trade.

2. *The village is not well served by public transport.* The local bus service now operates a two-hourly service to Milltown. There is no railway station. There is a canal which runs from North-West to South-East skirting the village. It is partially navigable being suitable for light craft but too silted for barges.

3. *There is an open air pool on the North bank of the River Lee.* This is open from May to the end of September. It is now run by Milltown Leisure Development following the introduction of competitive contract tendering.

4. *Edney Down United play in the Milltown Brewery League*. The club is thriving and their facilities are excellent. This is mainly due to the efforts of the Club Chair, Alison Moore, who has raised the local profile of the team and has attracted sponsorship from Marcol Holdings, the developers of the Milltown industrial estate. The clubhouse has been refurbished with the help of an interest free loan from the Milltown Brewery.

5. There is *one hotel in the village*, the Edney Arms, which is a 17th century coaching inn. It is located on the High Street. The proprietors, Michael and Janet Parsons, have recently opened a new, fashionable restaurant which has been awarded a rosette in the *Egon Ronay Guide*. They are anxious to develop the hotel and have approached the English Tourist Board for advice and assistance with their marketing.

6. *Carlton House is situated in a prime location* on the corner of the High Street and Market Square. It is a property which has been empty for two years and was formerly a bookshop. It is available to let on a five-year, renewable lease and is equipped with counters, telephone, mains electricity and ample storage space on the ground floor.

7. Lord Gwynne is anxious that the village should retain its image of being a *small rural community*. He is Chair of the Parish Council. He is only too aware of the need for the village to survive and believes that the solution to its future lies in small-scale tourism development.

8. Other members of the Parish Council are concerned that *tourism would be too seasonal*. They see the future of the village as lying in the development of a leisure complex on Chisholms. There are, however, many local residents who are opposed to planned development of any kind.

■ **TASKS**

1 Working in pairs and using the information provided in the scenario, produce a scale map or model of the village.

2 Produce a development plan for a leisure complex on Chisholms.

3 Produce an alternative plan for tourism development rather than leisure development, taking into account any objections which might be raised by environmental groups such as the Ramblers Association or the Countryside Commission.

4 The Parish Council is meeting to discuss the problems which the village faces. The Council is divided as to whether or not the village should be developed. It has been decided to hold an open meeting in the village hall. The development consortium and residents of Edney Down have been invited to attend. Prepare a speech to make at the meeting expressing opinions either in favour or in opposition to proposals for development.

5 You are a newspaper reporter working on the Milltown and District Times. Write a newspaper article which highlights the arguments put forward in the meeting. You should also take into consideration the feelings of the village community.

6a Write a letter from the owners of the Edney Arms Hotel to the English Tourist Board asking for marketing support.

b Using a copy of the Annual Report of the English Tourist Board, write a letter outlining ways in which the English Tourist Board would be able to help.

7 Taking into account the existing facilities in the village, prepare a business plan to present to the manager of the local bank for a commercial enterprise to be located in Carlton House.

EXPERIENCE ATTRACTIONS

Experience Attractions such as the *Jorvik Centre* in York or *Launch Pad* at the Science Museum in London give the visitor a sensory or physical experience by recreating situations relating to an event, location or theme. They are not museums but often incorporate a museum, gallery or other attraction as a secondary facility. Their aim is to increase visitor interest through interactive displays. The experiences are generally active rather than passive. They usually include either a ride and/or a 'Sensaround' experience. Events are presented in a series of tableaux or, where space permits, a guided tour will be presented by performers.

The following are examples of Experience Attractions:

- Ride experiences: *Jorvik Centre, Oxford Story*
- Sensaround: *Rock Circus, Stratford Experience*
- Hands-on experience: *Launch Pad*
- Performance attractions: *Wigan Pier, Granada Studio Tours*
- Factory experiences: *Sellafield, Cadbury World*
- Museum experiences: *Beamish, Black Country Museum, Gloddfa Ganol Slate Mine*

Experience Attractions are designed to provide a historical/cultural experience for the whole family. Most attractions are quite small as they are located in urban areas where space is at a premium. They are usually located in historic towns and cities or in areas looking to develop new leisure facilities. They require a large catchment to attract upwards of 200,000 visitors per year.

There are some 45 Experience attractions in the UK (see Table 1). The attractions are relatively new so that statistical data on visitor trends are inconclusive, but see Tables 2, 3 and 4.

The use of technology means that the attractions can, in principle, be managed with few staff although maintenance costs can be high. Performance attractions are staff intensive but displays can be easily and rapidly altered, encouraging repeat business.

Experience Attractions are expensive to build (see Table 5) and updating these attractions may also be expensive.

■ TASKS

1 It has been suggested that an Experience Attraction should be opened in a large town near where you live. You have been asked to put forward a proposal which would promote an aspect of the cultural life or heritage of the area.

Produce an outline theme for consideration. This may be related to the significance and achievements of a local industry, historical attraction, event or person or aimed at promoting a new technological concept.

2 Using the information provided, produce a report on what you consider to be the future of Experience Attractions.

For discussion

Do Experience Attractions promote aspects of culture and history or do they trivialise the work of museums and galleries?

For research

What are the most popular forms of Experience Attraction? Do the results which you have obtained from your own market research match any published statistics which you have found?

Table 1: Size of Heritage Experience Industry

	England	Rest of UK	Total UK
Heritage Experience Attractions	12	5	17
Hands-on Experience Attractions	12	2	14
Museum and Factory Experiences	11	3	14
Total 'Experiences'	35	10	45

Table 2: Visitor Numbers

Heritage Experience Attractions
1990 Visits ('000)

Jorvik, York	846
Granada Studio Tours, Manchester	600
Wigan Pier, Wigan	500
Tales of Robin Hood, Nottingham	179
Plymouth Dome, Plymouth	190
Morwellham Quay, Tavistock	125
Scotch Whisky Heritage Centre, Edinburgh	131
New Lanark Visitor Centre, Lanark	104

Museum Experiences

National Museum of Photography, Bradford	738
Museum of the Moving Image (MOMI), London	547
National Railway Museum, York	519
Mary Rose, Portsmouth	333
Black Country Museum, Dudley	304
Big Pit Mining Museum, Blaenavon	112
Inveraray Jail, Inveraray	104

Factory Experiences
1990 Visits ('000)

Cadbury World, Birmingham	185
Sellafield Visitor Centre, Sellafield	132

Hands-on Centres
Free-standing   **1989 Visits ('000)**

Exploratory Hands-on Science Centre, Bristol	200

Part of larger museum or attraction

Launch Pad, Science Museum, London	1,121
The Magician's Road National Railway Museum, York	543
Light on Science, Museum of Science & Industry, Birmingham	357
Xperiment! Museum of Science & Industry, Greater Manchester	252
Jodrell Bank Science Centre, Macclesfield	146
Technology Testbed, Big Objects Museum, Liverpool	83
Science Factory, Museum of Science & Engineering	

Source: British Tourist Authority

Table 3: Visitor Trends

| | *Visits pa* | | |
	1987	*1989*	*1990*
Jorvik	887	904	846
Wigan Pier (approx. estimates)	350	500	500
Royalty & Empire	371	335	–
Morwellham Quay	143	145	125
Exploratory hands-on Science Centre	86	101	200

Source: British Tourist Authority

Table 4: Admission Price Trends

| | *Ave. adult admission £'s* | | |
	1985	*1988*	*1990*
Wigan Pier (approx. estimates)	–	2.00	5.00
Morwellham Quay	(1986) 3.20	4.15	4.90
Llechwedd Slate Caverns	2.00	2.55	3.25
Jorvik	2.00	2.75	3.00
Oxford Story	–	3.00	3.00
Exploratory	–	2.00	3.00
Canterbury Tales	–	3.00	2.50
Scotch Whisky Heritage Centre	–	2.50	2.50

Source: British Tourist Authority

Table 5: Capital Costs and Funding

	Total (£m)	*Grants £'000*
White Cliffs Experience	10.00	NK
Granada Studio Tours	8.0	750
Cadbury World	5.5	NK
Royal Britain	5.0	200
Jorvik	2.7	250
Oxford Story	2.45	550
Edinburgh Story (abandoned)	2.3	NK
Scotch Whisky Heritage Centre	2.0	NK
Knights Caverns	2.0	NK
Tales of Robin Hood	1.7	200
Canterbury Tales	1.35	225
Rob Roy & Trossachs Visitor Centre	1.2	NK
Royalty & Empire - purchased as going concern for about	0.5	NK

NK = Not known

Leisure organisation

■ TASK 1

Nina Lauder, an International Perfume House have asked your organisation, Conference Planners Ltd to tender for the planning of a two day conference to be held in May/June next year to mark the launch of a new fragrance.

The client hopes to promote the new product internationally and therefore has shown an interest in holding the conference at a European resort. Top distributors and potential clients in addition to trade, national and international press are to be invited.

The specification for the tender is as follows:
On the first day there will be a presentation on the company, including its past achievements, short-term plans and current products. There will be presentations by the marketing and sales divisions which will include staging, videos and computer-generated graphics. This will culminate in a gala dinner where they will show their new product. Everyone will be given a sample range of the new product, including perfume, eau de toilette, bath and body lines.

The second day will include more presentations and highlight the advantages to the distributors and potential clients. Promotions planned for the coming year include; gift with purchase, special events on selected department stores, product support by tv and radio, point-of-sale material and training for consultants. This will culminate with dinner at a venue of local interest.

You are to prepare the tender taking into consideration the following: a budget of £40k, one hundred delegates to be invited, forty Nina Lauder staff, the venue and its facilities, transport and transfer arrangements, equipment, itinerary, gala dinner and other meals.

Nina Lauder are looking for conference planners with initiative and innovative ideas.

■ TASK 2

Scenario

1993   You are planning to open a small business in Leisure Studies.

1995   The business has been operational for two years, and has been a great success. You employ three people, and frequently have more business enquiries than you can help. You have quite a small office space, and whilst you could expand, lack of capital prevents this.

During an exhibition you meet someone in the same line of business who is looking for new premises in order to expand. After several meetings, and completion of certain formalities you enter into a partnership together, jointly financing the purchase of new premises. The business continues to thrive and most of your profits are ploughed back into the business. You are aware that there is a building next door which is for sale, and would be ideal for expansion.

1988   After much consultation you decide to form a private limited company, changing your name in accordance with the law. The venture is a big success and after a few years the owners realise the limitations of a private limited company.

2000   After a few years of continued success it is decided that the next step is to become a public limited company.

1   Briefly describe the main advantages and disadvantages of operating as a:

    a   sole trader
    b   partnership
    c   private limited company
    d   public limited company

Show how the accounting procedure would differ in each operation when distributing the annual profit, giving an example of each.

2   Identify the methods of raising finance in 1993, 1995, 1998 and 2000.

3   Describe two of the major documents which would be sent to the Registrar of Companies.

4   Prepare a detailed report to submit to the shareholders emphasising the advantages of 'going public'. Note: this should be in report style, not letter or memo etc.

5   Investigate the possibilities of operating a franchise, listing the advantages and disadvantages to the franchisor, franchisee and customer.

6   Through you own research list four companies and the product/service they provide which would fall into the categories listed in question 1.

Communication in the leisure industry

■ TASK 1

The Leisure Industry covers a wide range of facilities, activities, outlets and occupations.

1   Using a map of your local area pinpoint where you can locate the leisure outlets listed below:

- Swimming pool
- Sports centre
- Leisure centre
- Theatre
- Cinema
- Bingo hall
- Night club
- Public house
- Wine bar
- Restaurant

2   Gather information on each outlet to include admission prices, availability, facilities, opening times etc.

3   Visit two establishments from the list and with permission prepare a profile of the staff employed. What qualifications do they possess? What experience have they? Have they always worked in the leisure industry? How many hours do they each work? Is it shift work? Are staff employed on a seasonal basis?

■ TASK 2

Mr Brian Murphy is about to open a Sports Shop in your town. He has just purchased a lease on a property close to the centre, and is currently trying to reorganise the layout of the premises, which were formerly a Building Society. The office he intends to use as the outlet measures 54' × 14'. It is currently little more than a shell and he feels it necessary to ensure that the layout of the office promotes job satisfaction for the five people that will be employed.

He advertised for a trainee manager and appointed Ms Susan Stryker, aged 21. Susan is new to the area and will be looking for accommodation. It is possible for her to purchase a flat as she has a deposit of £20,000 and will be earning £11,000.

1 Carry out research into office equipment, decorations, carpeting, furnishings etc, for Mr Murphy that will promote a good environment for his staff and members of the public.

2 Make a plan to scale of an office, with furniture, equipment etc.

3 Write a report giving your reasons for the layout, and suggest how the offices should be decorated, lit, carpeted etc.

4 What aspects of the Offices, Shops and Railway Premises Act 1963 and Health and Safety at Work Act 1974 must be included in the planning of the new office?

5 Explain what protection is given in law to the customer under the Trade Descriptions Act 1968.

6 Identify the needs of Ms Stryker, e.g. accommodation, entertainment, range of facilities.

■ TASK 3

Collect the following information in order to produce a series of visual interpretations of data, comparing facilities and services.

Compare the different features of two hotels in your local area, including at least:

1 History of the hotel and other hotels within the group
2 No. of rooms and room types
3 No. of guests
4 Average lengths of stay
5 Room rates
6 Types of customer e.g. business/holiday etc.
7 Facilities in a standard room
8 No. of staff
9 Hotel services
10 Exchange rates

Select two sports centres and complete a similar comparison.

Keep a record of all your correspondence and telephone calls and include them in your findings and presentations. Display the information in the form of graphs, charts, tables and flow charts as applicable.

Give an oral presentation to the rest of your group outlining your findings.

■ TASK 4

Visit two leisure centres, one which uses Electronic Technology (ET) extensively and one which has limited facilities (use your work placement as one).

Find out what ET is used by the organisations and what impact these facilities have had on the day-to-day running of the establishment, both for the people involved and the organisation.

1   Make appointments at the chosen establishments.

2   Prepare a questionnaire.

3   Visit the establishments to collect information.

4   Write a report of your findings, which should include a comparison of both sets of establishment. At least one page should be completed using ET. Include all your research.

■ TASK 5

Under current legislation an employee (subject to certain exceptions) has the right not to be dismissed unfairly and may seek a remedy by complaining.

1   Consider the legal aspects.

2   Research the procedures, and submit a chart, illustrating the steps which are followed before a case can be heard at an Industrial Tribunal.

3   Sit in on an Industrial Tribunal hearing and submit a report on your opinions on the case heard, and a summary of the case.

4   Produce a code of practice handbook to be given to future students in your department.

Finance

■ TASK 1

The following trial balance was prepared for Mega Sports on 31 March 1992. The balances failed to agree. Re-write and correct the trial balance.

	Credit	Debit
Purchases		74900
Sales	80800	
Rent and rates	2989	
Light and heat		1477
Stock	8313	
Wages	11074	
Insurance		472
Premises		155000
Fixtures	3500	
General expenses		1770
Debtors	11080	
Creditors	4221	
Cash at bank		13460
Equipment	8400	
Vehicles		19250
Motor expenses		3986
Capital	230650	
	361027	270315

Give two examples of where a trial balance may balance but may still be incorrect.

■ TASK 2

Mr Evan Wyburn opened an exciting sports venture on 1 January 1991. Record the transactions for his first month, double balance each account and complete a trial balance.

Jan 1   Started business with a capital of £3500, made up of £3000 in the bank and £500 cash

Jan 2   Bought tennis balls, shuttlecocks and other light equipment by cheque for £150

Jan 3   Bought table tennis tables, lockers and towels on credit from L. Christie £360, S. Gunnell £490, L. Piggot £110, D. Broome £340

Jan 3   Cash sales £95

Jan 4   Bought goods for cash £35

Jan 4   Bought stationery from Rymans £170

Jan 4   Sold goods on credit to B. Becker £90, M. Navratilova £150, C. Evert £190, M. Stich £160

Jan 5   Paid rent by cheque £55

Jan 6   Bought shoe racks and clothes horses on credit from E. Goolagong £480

Jan 7   Paid salaries in cash £120

Jan 8   Bought motor vehicle from Goodmayes Motor on credit for £700

Jan 8   Received loan from F. Perry by cheque £600

Jan 9   Cash sales £190

Jan 10   Sold goods on credit to M. Navratilova £100, M. Stich £340 and V. Wade £115

Jan 11   Received cheques from V. Wade £115 and M. Navratilova for £250

Jan 12   Paid the following by cheque – S. Gunnell £450 and L. Piggot £50

Jan 14   Received a further loan from F. Perry for £200 cash

Jan 15   C. Evert returned goods valued at £15

Jan 17   Received £500 from M. Stich by cheque

Jan 18   Returned goods to E Goolagong £30

Jan 20   Bought another Motor van for cash for £500

Jan 22   Banked cash sales £450

Jan 29   Sold goods on credit to S. Smith £100 and I. Nastase £200

Jan 31   Bought goods on credit from I. Botham £10

Jan 31   Mr Wyburn decided that he had worked extremely hard for the whole month dealing with students on work experience and so drew £4400 from the bank for his own use.

Explain the balance in the bank account. What do you notice?

■ TASK 3

Explain and give examples of the following:

- Credit sales
- Cash sales
- Assets
- Liabilities
- Debtors and creditors

■ TASK 4

1 Make arrangements to visit the local office of the Inland Revenue to collect samples of the following documents:

- P60
- P45
- P46

2 Calculate the net pay for the following employees using the current figures as outlined in the Chancellor's Budget (tax and N.I.):

a Ms N Bradshaw is a Recreational Assistant earning £19 500 p.a. She is not married and has a six year old daughter. Calculate her monthly pay.

b Mr de Freitas is a swimming instructor earning £17 800 per year. Calculate his weekly pay.

3 Describe in detail and give examples of the following:

- Premium hours pay
- Danger money
- Overtime
- Piece rates
- Commission
- Tax codes
- Tax allowances

Sport and physical recreation

■ TASK 1

You have recently finished your work experience at a local junior school where you were involved with pupils from each year, both boys and girls.

As part of your training programme the P.E. teacher has asked you to design a new activity (game) suitable for a class of 15–20 pupils, to be played either on an individual or a team basis.

Present this information in the form of an assignment, giving specific times, instructions, rules of play, objectives and criteria for successful completion of this game.

Illustrate your assignment by means of a detailed plan, diagram and system of allocating points.

It is hoped that some of the activities will be selected by the school, and that under direction and supervision by the creator, will be carried out in a local school.

■ TASK 2

You have recently been appointed recreational officer for a Local Authority and your first major task is the planning, design and development of a children's playground.

Having consulted local planners you have discovered that the location is on the site of a former factory, and widespread clearance has resulted in a large area of open space. It is close to a number of schools and shops.

Your role is to consult with the local community and then proceed to design a playground which will be safe and easily maintained. Clearly, safety is of paramount importance and should include equipment safety, and ease of supervision, e.g. no blind spots.

■ TASK 3

List all the facilities for water recreation in your local area including indoor and outdoor, formal and informal. Name the provider of each activity e.g. public, private or voluntary organisations.

Research and write an illustrated report on water recreation in your area which takes into account the following:

- a detailed description of each facility;
- the advantages and disadvantages to the community of at least one of the facilities;
- compare and contrast two or more swimming pools with regard to maintenance, hygiene, safety, technology, staffing, activities;
- prepare a user profile comparing different activities.

Countryside

■ TASK

Select one organisation from each of the following sectors:

Public sector

- Countryside Commission
- National Parks
- Forestry Commission
- Nature Conservancy Council
- British Waterways Board
- Regional Water Authorities
- Sports Council
- English Heritage

Private sector

- Safari/Wildlife Parks
- Caravan/Camping sites
- Park Owners
- Farm landlords
- Estate Owners

Voluntary sector

- Outward Bound Trust
- Youth Hostel Association
- National Trust
- Camping Club of Great Britain and Ireland
- Ramblers Association
- Central Foundation for Physical Recreation

1   Research and write a detailed report explaining and comparing the objectives, roles and activities of the organisations you have selected. It should be approximately 1500 words in length and be illustrated with photos, maps graphs etc.

2   Give a short verbal report on one of your selected organisations.

Marketing

■ **TASK 1**

You are currently employed in a large leisure complex, situated in the Lake District, that has decided to market special activity weekends as follows:

- fishing
- golf
- rambling
- artist
- gourmet

1 Design a short advertisement to place in a newspaper or magazine.

2 Suggest a suitable specialist magazine for each of the activity weekends to be advertised in.

3 Cost the advert for both a one-off and a series of adverts in a national newspaper and a specialist magazine.

4 Design a suitable package, commencing with dinner on Friday and ending with afternoon tea on Sunday for at least one of the activity weekends.

■ **TASK 2**

Investigate the advantages and disadvantages of adding leisure facilities to an existing hospitality operation, e.g. an hotel.

What marketing ideas can you think of that would increase business and give a good capital return?

Design an organisation chart for a leisure complex within an hotel, and show which roles may have twin responsibilities.

With permission, research information using a questionnaire on the feasibility of a leisure centre within an hotel that currently has no such provision.

Finance and marketing

■ TASK

A charity record-breaking aerobics class is to be organised by your college in conjunction with the local authority. The event is to be held at the local football stadium and because of the number of people involved and the attempt to break a record, security and marshalls will have to be employed.

Under these conditions there must be at least 30 marshalls if 4500 or less people wish to participate. For each 60 extra people between 4500 and 6000 there needs to be one extra marshall and the same for each 40 extra people over 6000 up to a maximum of 7500. Each marshall will be paid £5.

To participate will cost £2.

The cost of lighting, administrative staff etc are to be paid regardless of the number of people participating and amount to £1000.

Those participating will be given a drink and a bar of chocolate at the end of the event and these will be provided by Marz Chocolates at cost price, on a sale or return at 20p each person.

The sound system will be provided at a reduced rate of £350.

In order for people to be aware of the event it needs to be advertised. Capital Radio are assisting with this and are providing posters at 10p each, together with adverts in tube stations at £30 and on the radio at a discounted rate of £75. It has been estimated that to attract 3000 participants it is necessary to spend £150 on posters, and £600 on newspaper ads. The radio, it is estimated, will attract the following:

1st ad – 1000 more tickets
2nd ad – 500 more tickets
3rd ad – 250 more tickets
4th ad – 50 more tickets
5th ad – 30 more tickets
Additional ads will each attract 20 people.

What are the fixed and variable costs of the event? How many people are to participate in order to break even? What amount is raised for charity at total capacity? How much advertising should be carried out?

Provide a full written analysis and break even chart. Either prepare a radio jingle suitable for advertising and present this in the form of an audio cassette *or* design a newspaper and poster advert and give comprehensive details of where it should be displayed.

Arts, entertainment and tourism

■ TASK 1

The Passion Play, Oberammergau, is held every ten years. What is it? Your investigations should include:

1 a thorough account of the history of this event
2 its location
3 who is involved
4 how long each performance lasts
5 when the performance begins.

Having completed the above, you are employed in a Travel Agency in your home town. A client has requested information on transport to the play and needs your assistance. There are four people travelling in the group, two adults and two children, one aged five and one aged fifteen. Using a variety of sources ascertain the best route and calculate the most suitable total fare for the family to see the performance. Accommodation is not necessary.

■ TASK 2

The college has decided to hold a karaoke party towards the end of the academic year. Management have approached the leisure students and asked them to organise, promote and carry out the event to include college staff and friends, at a small fee to cover costs.

1 Nominate a committee and allocate responsibilities as appropriate.

2 Design promotional material.

3 Design a ticket, check the cost of printing and then produce the required amount.

4 Compile a programme of events.

5 Arrange meetings with course tutors and college committees to discuss progress and report from each section of the student committee.

6 Carry out the project.

7 Prepare a break even analysis to demonstrate its profitability to include:

    a what are the fixed and variable costs for the event

    b how many tickets must be sold to break even

    c how many tickets should be sold to make maximum profit.

8 Briefly analyse the event and the students' roles on the committee.

Working in the leisure industry

■ TASK 1

As a new recruit to Conference Planners Ltd you have been asked to produce a comprehensive guide to conference venues in the South of England. The guide should include information on facilities available and list the advantages of each venue.

The completed package will be initially distributed to tourist offices in the South East and also high profile international companies with the intention of overseas marketing in the future.

■ TASK 2

During your work experience programme it is essential that you maintain a weekly diary outlining your training, a description of the organisation and its position in the leisure market.

1   What hospitality function is provided e.g. food and beverage and/or accommodation. Give a detailed description of the services available. If none exist, complete a feasibility study that highlights the possibilities of such a function and give your recommendations.

2   Identify the different methods of payment for customers/clients/guests. What are the advantages to the organisation and the customer of each type of payment. It may help to display your information in the form of charts and diagrams.

3   What rules and regulations govern the employers in relation to staffing, i.e. equal opportunities, ethnic minorities, disabled employees, disciplinary rules etc.

4   With permission, arrange to collect a portfolio of specimen documents (letters, forms, etc.) which your organisation currently uses. Explain for what purpose each is used. Or, if possible, arrange to look at some sample personnel job specifications and job descriptions used within your organisation. Shadow one of the jobs and keep a task-by-task record of what actually takes place.

5 In no more than five hundred words give details of the history of the organisation, its main competitors and its plan for development giving consideration to the development of the European Community.

6 Complete a customer/client profile. Explain how the results of your survey could be useful to the management of the organisation.

7 Give a thorough explanation of the sporting activities/ courses/clubs within the organisation. If none exist, survey the staff to identify social pastimes and leisure activities.

■ TASK 3

1 Prepare a letter to prospective bankers outlining plans for setting up a small leisure business.

2 Prepare a business plan estimating costs, cash flow forecasts and budgets.

3 Prepare a list of the legal requirements that will have to be considered prior to opening a new establishment.

4 Produce advertising and promotional material for the establishment.

GLOSSARY OF SOME COMMONLY USED FINANCIAL TERMS

Accumulated reserve The net worth of an organisation.

Asset Property that has a value and may be sold to pay a debt.

Balance sheet A summary of the financial state of a business which highlights how the business has used its resources over a period of time and lists assets, sources of funds, liabilities, and working capital.

Capital expenditure Major expenditure, such as buildings, equipment or the freehold of a property.

Cash flow projection A forecast of items of anticipated income and expenditure.

Current assets Assets that could be sold within a year if required.

Current liabilities Debts to other people or organisations that will need to be repaid within the coming year.

Debenture A form of secured loan, usually offering a fixed rate of interest.

Debt Money or goods owed to someone else.

Deferred loan A loan – usually relating to capital projects – on which repayment does not begin until after completion of the project.

Depreciation A mechanism for writing off the cost or value of an asset over its useful life. It is applied particularly to items such as vehicles and equipment.

Dividend A share of profits paid to shareholders.

Fixed assets Assets of a more permanent nature, such as buildings, that may not be easily sold or otherwise disposed of.

Inflation The cumulative effect of rising prices, usually expressed as a percentage.

Lease An agreement to use equipment in exchange for rent. The rental is paid over a fixed term, at the end of which the user may have the option to buy the equipment or take out another lease agreement.

Liquid assets Items that can be easily sold or realised at short notice, including cash, some investments on 'short call' and stocks.

Mortgage A *secured property* loan.

Profit and loss account An account used to calculate the net profit or loss earned during a specified period. It should be used in conjunction with a *balance sheet*. The account shows operating costs against revenue income. It will usually show specific items, such as staff costs, loan repayments, insurance premiums and maintenance costs.

Revenue expenditure Expenditure that is of a recurring nature, such as business rates, electricity and so on.

Share capital The value of all shares issued by a company.

Stock in hand Usable stock that remains unsold at the end of a trading period but which may be sold at the commencement of the next trading period.

Value Added Tax (VAT) An indirect tax that is charged on goods and services in the course of business. Organisations that are liable for VAT (currently 17.5 per cent) must register with the Customs and Excise Department.

Working capital The difference between *current liabilities* and *current assets*.

USEFUL ADDRESSES

■ GOVERNMENT

Department of the Environment
Sport and Recreation Division
Marsham Street
London SW1P 3EB
Tel: 071–276 3000

Department of National Heritage
Government Offices
Great George Street
London SW1P 3AL
Tel: 071–240 6000 *or* 5811

The Civil Service Commission
Alencon Link
Basingstoke
Hampshire RG21 1JB

Local Government Training Board
Arndale House
The Arndale Centre
Luton
Bedfordshire LU1 2TS

■ ART AND ENTERTAINMENT

The Arts Council of Great Britain
14 Great Peter Street
London SW1P 3NQ
Tel: 071–333 0100

The Arts Council of Northern Ireland
181A Stranmillis Road
Belfast BT9 5DU

Association of British Theatre Technicians
4–7 Great Pulteney Street
London W1V 0AV

The British Broadcasting Corporation
Broadcasting House
Portland Place
London W1A 1AA

The British Council
11 Portland Place
London W1N 4EJ

The Independent Broadcasting Authority
70 Brompton Road
London SW3 1EY

Library Association
7 Ridgemount Street
London WC1E 7AE

Museum and Galleries Commission
16 Queen Anne's Gate
London SW1H 9AA

The Scottish Arts Council
12 Manor Place
Edinburgh EH3 7DD

The Welsh Arts Council
Holst House
Museum Place
Cardiff CF1 3NX

■ COUNTRYSIDE

The Association of Countryside Rangers
The Bunting
Kingsley
Stoke-on-Trent
Staffordshire ST10 2AZ

The British Trust for Conservation Volunteers
The London Ecology Centre
80 York Way
London N1 9AG

The Council for the Protection of Rural England
Warwick House
25 Buckingham Palace Road
London SW1W 0PP

The Countryside Commission
John Dower House
Crescent Place
Cheltenham
Gloucestershire GL50 3RA
Tel: 0242 521381

The Countryside Commission for Scotland
Battleby
Redgorton
Perth PH1 3EW

The Countryside Council for Wales
Plas Renrhos
Ffordd
Renrhos
Bangor LL57 2LQ

The Forestry Commission
231 Corstorphine Road
Edinburgh EH12 7AT
Tel: 031-334 0303

Inland Waterways Association
114 Regents Park Road
London NW1 8UQ

The National Trust
36 Queen Anne's Gate
London SW1H 9AS
Tel: 071-222 9251

The National Trust for Scotland
5 Charlotte Square
Edinburgh EH2 4DU

The Nature Conservancy Council
Northminster House
Peterborough
Cambridgeshire PE1 1UA
Tel: 0733 40345

The Ramblers' Association
1/5 Wandsworth Road
London SW8 2XX

Royal Society for the Protection of Birds
The Lodge
Sandy
Bedfordshire SG19 2DL

The Wildfowl and Wetlands Trust
Slimbridge
Gloucester GL2 7BT

■ SPORT AND PHYSICAL RECREATION

British Olympic Association
1 Wandsworth Plain
London SW18 1EH

British Sports Association for the Disabled
34 Osnaburgh Street
London NW1 3ND

Central Council of Physical Recreation
Francis House
Francis Street
London SW1P 1DE

The Institute of Baths and Recreation Management
Gifford House
36–38 Sherrard Street
Melton Mowbray
Leicestershire LE13 1XJ

The Institute of Leisure and Amenity Management
Lower Basildon
Reading
Berkshire RG8 9NE

The Institute of Sports Sponsorship
Francis House
Francis Street
London SW1P 1DE

National Children's Play and Recreation Unit
359–361 Euston Road
London NW1 3AL

The National Playing Fields Association
25 Ovington Square
London SW3 1LQ
Tel: 071–584 6445

Recreation Managers Association
5 Balfour Road
Weybridge
Surrey KT13 8HE

Scottish Sports Council
Caledonia House
South Gyle
Edinburgh EH12 9DQ

The Sports Aid Foundation
16 Upper Woburn Place
London WC1H 0QN

The Sports Council
16 Upper Woburn Place
London WC1H 0QP
Tel: 071-388 1277

The Sports Council for Wales
The National Sports Centre for Wales
Sophia Gardens
Cardiff CF1 9SW
Tel: 0222 381222

■ TOURISM

The Association of British Travel Agents
National Training Board
7–11 Chertsey Road
Woking
Surrey GU21 5AL

The English Tourist Board
Thames Tower
Black's Road
London W6 9EL
Tel: 071–846 9000

The British Tourist Authority
Thames Tower
Black's Road
London W6 9EL
Tel: 071–846 9000

The Institute of Travel and Tourism
113 Victoria Street
St Albans
Hertfordshire

The London Tourist Board
26 Grosvenor Gardens
London SW1 0DU
Tel: 071–730 3450

The Tourism Society
26 Grosvenor Gardens
London SW1 0DU

The Wales Tourist Board
8–14 Bridge Street
Cardiff CF1 2EE
Tel: 0222 227281

■ EDUCATION

Business and Technician Education Council
Central House
Upper Woburn Place
London WC1H 0HH
Tel: 071–413 8400

City and Guilds of London Institute
76 Portland Place
London W1N 4AA
Tel: 071–580 3050

The Royal Society of Arts Examination Board
Westwood Way
Westwood Business Park
Coventry CV4 8HS
Tel: 0203 470033

INDEX